Secrets

RESTAURANT

*Featuring a collection of recipes
and gift certificates from the best
restaurants in the area*

presented by

CUC INTERNATIONAL

Cover photo by Michael A. Gallitelli

Have you ever dined in a restaurant and tried to make the same meal at home but it was... different?
Upon asking the restaurant for the recipe, you heard... "it's a secret."
Well, not anymore...

Welcome to "Restaurant Secrets" Collection Series, Volume I
featuring a collection of 50 treasured recipes from the best restaurants in the area.

Since the beginning of time, a meal has been the universal activity that transcends
all languages and ethnic backgrounds. A grand meal is the canvas for celebrations of love and friendship.
A fine dining experience soothes the soul, nurtures the mind, and warms the heart.
"Restaurant Secrets" brings you the great meals from the kitchens of the best restaurants in the area,
and teaches you to cook like a chef in your own home.

Expert restaurateurs have taken great care in preparing their famous recipes, including every ingredient and
preparation step, so that you can easily experience the same extraordinary results at home.
You are cordially invited to "Test the Chef" with the enclosed gift certificates
and see how your versions compare to the pros!

Discover the wisdom of the area's best restaurateurs as you taste and enjoy their recipes in your own kitchen.
When a guest asks you, "What's your secret?" remember to tell them that it's not a secret anymore.

"Restaurant Secrets" Collection Series, Volume I...
Great for cooking at home, dining out, or giving as a gift!

Happy Cooking and Fine Dining!

Table of Contents

Restaurants

Kid Friendly

Banquet Facilities

HeartSmart Menu

Credit Cards Accepted

Valet Parking

Alcohol Served

RESTAURANT Secrets® of Milwaukee

MILWAUKEE IS CULINARY RICH

Milwaukee's rich heritage dates back to the early 1800's. A blending of many ethnic backgrounds has blessed the city with a wide variety of cultural attractions. One of Milwaukee's best known attractions is the quality of independent restaurants, each with a rich heritage all its own. Milwaukee is known worldwide as being a culinary rich city, unequaled with uniqueness and never out done by quality. We are proud to have Milwaukee's best restaurants unified together in *Restaurant Secrets of Milwaukee*. Each restaurant took a lot of pride in choosing the right recipe for this publication. The same pride goes into every entree prepared daily by many talented, trained chefs. Many of the restaurants in *Restaurant Secrets* belong to the Wisconsin Restaurant Association Milwaukee Chapter. Because of their participation in this community project, a portion of the proceeds from some of the sales of this edition will go back to the Milwaukee Chapter to help train and educate future Milwaukee chefs.

We would like to thank the Restaurant Secrets independent restaurants of Milwaukee, their talented chefs and staff for their contributions to enhancing the quality of life in our great city.

We encourage you to support these restaurants with your patronage.

Grenadier's
747 N. Broadway
Milwaukee, WI
(414) 276-0747

Grenadier's

If you have not experienced dining at Grenadier's yet, you have not enjoyed the true meaning of dining out.
Excellent food created by Knut Apitz, Charles Weber and their staff has impressed the toughest food connoisseur.
The elegant service and gracious atmosphere will allow you to realize why Grenadier's is a recipient of many local
and national awards in Wisconsin. We welcome your visit and look forward to adding your name to our list of
satisfied diners — which is the same list we call "friends." Open Monday through Friday for lunch and Monday
through Saturday for dinner. Closed Sunday. Call 276-0747 for reservations. Visit us at our Websight
http://www.Foodspot.com/Grenadiers/

Tapenade Crusted Chilean Sea Bass with Fettuccini

Preparation:

1. Season sea bass with salt and pepper, spread an even layer of Tapenade across the entire top of the fish.

2. Bake fish under a broiler for 6 to 8 minutes depending on the thickness of the fish.

3. While fish is cooking, assemble sautéed peppers and tomatoes over the fettuccini in a large entree bowl.

4. Serve fish over pasta.

5. Finish dish with basil oil and fresh basil.

Directions:

1. In a food processor, combine all crust ingredients except bread crumbs and olive oil.

2. Blend until smooth, then add bread crumbs, blend again.

3. Slowly add olive oil while blending, add enough to reach a smooth paste like consistency - it should not look oily.

4. Reserve until needed - keep refrigerated.

6 6 ounce pieces of boneless, skinless sea bass
2 cups tapenade mixture from below
8 cups cooked fettuccini
1 each red, yellow, and green pepper-julienned
4 each ripe Roma tomatoes, julienned
6 tablespoons fresh basil, chiffonade
12 ounces basil flavored olive oil, (homemade or store bought) (use as much as you prefer)

Tapenade Crust
(3 Cups)
1 cup dry cured pitted black olives (nicoise olives optional)
1/4 cup capers-drained
10 pieces anchovies
2 tablespoons roasted garlic cloves
1 tablespoon fresh thyme leaves
1 tablespoon fresh rosemary leaves
olive oil as needed
1 small bunch parsley - leaves only
1 cup white bread crumbs

![PANDL'S IN BAYSIDE]

Pandl's In Bayside
8825 N. Lake Dr.
Bayside, WI
(414) 352-7300

Pandl's In Bayside opened in October 1968 and has been family owned and operated ever since. Voted best brunch in Milwaukee by local residents for the last 8 years straight. Selected as one of Milwaukee's most romantic restaurants by Fox's Channel 6. Enjoy the beautiful natural setting where wildlife is often seen throughout the year. Pandl's in Bayside features many items common to menus across Wisconsin, but each dish is prepared with skill and care and has resulted in a very loyal following.

One of our most popular dishes, scallops done the way they should be.

Scallops in Champagne Sauce with Penne

Method: In stainless steel or non-stick pot heat all sauce ingredients to simmer for 2 minutes. Slowly mix in approximately 2 teaspoons of roux or add until sauce is slightly thickened. Cook for five more minutes, then remove from heat and stir in parmesan cheese. Set aside.

Dust seasoned scallops in flour and sauté in clarified butter on all sides until just golden brown, then remove from pan. Then add diced vegetables and sauté for two minutes or until onion and leek start to become translucent. Pour off butter, add chablis and 2 cups of sauce, bring to simmer, add scallops, simmer 1/2 minute more. Remove scallops to plate as shown, add penne pasta to pan and heat pasta through. Spoon pasta to center of plate and garnish with parmesan cheese and chopped parsley.

*Dry-packed scallops have not been treated with preservatives or soaked to increase in size. They will appear dull and sticky at the market, not shiny and slippery. You may use treated scallops which are the typical frozen scallops in most markets. If you do, they may splatter in pan when sautéing and shrink slightly and lose some of the dusted flour.

Ingredients Sauce for 4 to 6

2 cups heavy cream

1 tablespoon lemon juice

1 cup champagne

2 bay leaves

pinch of ground cloves

white pepper and season salt to taste

Roux for Thickening

cooked, clarified butter/flour mixture (equal parts)

1/2 cup shredded parmesan cheese

Sauté Pan for 2 persons

1 ounce red peppers, diced

1 ounce white of leek, diced

1 ounce red onion, diced

2 ounces chablis

1/4 cup flour

1/8 cup clarified butter

2 cups cooked penne pasta

Garnish

1/8 cup shredded parmesan cheese

1/2 teaspoon diced parsley

*1 pound dry-packed scallops with side muscle removed, and lightly seasoned with salt and white pepper

Karl Ratzsch's

Karl Ratzsch's

THE IMPRESSIVE GERMAN RESTAURANT

Karl Ratzsch's
320 E. Mason
Milwaukee, WI
(414) 276-2720

Consistently voted Milwaukee's favorite German restaurant, Karl Ratzsch's is a tradition in Milwaukee. Housed within its walls is a priceless collection of German steins, porcelain and delicate hand painted glassware. The top tier German dishes all vie for your attention and the extensive selection of noble German wines served to complement the favorite German entrées. The Ratzsch family has owned and operated this establishment for three generations. Gemutlichkeit abounds at this DiRoNA award winner.

The Rheinlander Veal, our featured recipe, marries delicate sautéed veal with a delightful, savory mushroom and wine sauce.

A selection of any of our estate bottled Rieslings provides a natural rhyming to the elegance of this entrée.

Subtle nuances of shallots, mushrooms and wine inform this elegant veal sauté beckoning the "Old World".

Rheinlander Veal

Heat a large skillet on medium heat. Season and dredge veal cutlets in flour. Add 2 tablespoons butter and veal cutlets to skillet. Sauté veal about one minute per side and remove veal to warm plate. Using the same skillet, over medium heat, add shallots and mushrooms. Sauté 1 minute and deglaze skillet with Rhein wine and cook for 1 minute. Add veal stock and reduce to half. Whisk in 2 tablespoons of soft butter until sauce is slightly thickened. Remove from stove and adjust seasonings with salt and pepper. Spoon sauce over veal and garnish plate with puree of carrot and fresh steamed asparagus spears.

2 veal cutlets {3 ounce inside round slices} flattened to 1/8 inch

1 tablespoon diced shallots

one half cup veal stock

one quarter cup Rhein wine

5 tablespoons soft butter

salt to taste

fresh ground black pepper to taste

1 cup sliced mushrooms

1 cup flour

Ristorante Bartolotta
7616 W. State St.
Wauwatosa, WI
(414) 771-7910

What was once the Pabst Brewery Saloon at the turn of the century, is now Ristorante Bartolotta. Peter Piper's Pancake House and Harwood's were previous tenants at 7616 West State Street. Currently, Ristorante Bartolotta, a four-star dining hot spot, opened on March 22, 1993 and was instantly acclaimed by clientele and food critics as the Best New Restaurant of the Year. The reason is simple, Bartolotta's serves great Italian food prepared authentically and served in a quaint, romantically rustic atmosphere that feels more like Italy than Wauwatosa, Wisconsin. Owner, Joseph Bartolotta, prides himself on his simple, rustic recipes using the finest fresh ingredients which are the very soul of Italian food. Ristorante Bartolotta is a landmark to Milwaukee with its fine dining, award winning wine list, strong clientele and splendid cuisine.

Our fine cuisine is the responsibility of our Chef John Korycki. John started as a line cook at Spiaggia under Chef Paul Bartolotta, and was promoted to sous chef in a year's time. He realized and nurtured a passion for truly authentic Italian food. To foster his knowledge of Italian cuisine, John visited Italy twice. During his three month tour, John worked in several restaurants in different regions of Italy. Upon his return to the States, John relocated to Milwaukee to help open Lake Park Bistro as sous chef. He was then promoted to Executive Chef at Ristorante Bartolotta in October, 1996.

Ristorante Bartolotta serves lunch and dinner. Dinner reservations recommended.

Cornish hen roasted crisp, with rosemary, lemon and natural juices.

Polletto Alla Toscana

Prepare the Cornish hens by splitting them down the backbone and removing the breast bones. The wing tip bones and leg thigh bones may also be removed if desired. With the hen laying flat and skin side up, gently pound the breast and leg meat to flatten slightly.

Season the hens generously with salt and pepper. Sprinkle with olive oil and place in a medium hot skillet. Sauté the hens in olive oil, skin side down, until golden brown. Turn hens over and add the garlic and rosemary to the pan. Finish cooking the hens by roasting them in a 350 degree oven for 15-20 minutes or until thoroughly cooked.

To serve, squeeze the lemon over the hens and serve with the collected pan juices.

Serves 2-4.

At Bartolotta's we serve the Cornish hen accompanied with roasted rosemary potatoes and brussel sprouts caramelized in butter, olive oil and black pepper.

2 Cornish hens
(1-1/2 pounds each)

(A 3-1/2 pound chicken may be substituted)

2 ounces extra virgin olive oil

4 garlic cloves, halved

2 rosemary sprigs

1 lemon halved

coarse salt to taste

freshly ground coarse black pepper to taste

8

The Golden Mast
1270 Lacy Lane
Okauchee, WI
(414) 567-7047

Golden Mast Inn

Arriving here from the Black Forest area of Germany, Hans and Maria Weissgerber settled in Milwaukee in 1956 and opened their first family restaurant, The Golden Mast on Okauchee Lake in 1967. The ambiance of Wisconsin is reflected from the intimate view of Okauchee Lake at the Golden Mast. Beautifully appointed dining rooms with dramatic window walls invite classic lakeside dining. Memorable banquets and parties are held in our indoor/outdoor banquet facilities. Enjoy a scenic drive into the lake country area of Waukesha County and please your palates with a wonderful array of tasteful entrees. Serving daily: Mon.-Sat. 5 to 10pm., Sun. Brunch 11 to 2 pm and Dinner 4-9 pm.

A succulent blend of sautéed shrimp, boiled linguine and sun-ripened cherry tomatoes.

Shrimp Scampi

Cook linguine ahead of time and refrigerate. When serving, have a pot of hot water ready and drop linguine in to warm up. Remove and place on plate.

Heat sauté pan and add 4 tablespoons of your scampi butter. Then add 12 pieces of shrimp. Sauté slowly, when almost fully cooked you may adjust butter mixture, maybe 3 tablespoons. Also add bread crumbs and cherry tomatoes.

Have linguine heated and drained. Place on plate. Place 6 shrimp on top of linguine and pour some butter mixture over. Garnish.

Yield 2 servings.

12 raw peeled
and cleaned shrimp

1 package linguine

8 cherry tomatoes, halved

1/2 cup bread crumbs

<u>Blend together</u>

1/2 cup butter

1/2 cup margarine

1 tablespoon Worcestershire

1 tablespoon A-1 Sauce

1 tablespoon diced onion

1/4 teaspoon white pepper

1 teaspoon granulated garlic

1/4 teaspoon salt

drop Tabasco sauce

1/2 teaspoon tarragon

2 tablespoons grated
parmesan cheese

Refrigerate butter mixture

The Black Kettle
8660 N. 107th St.
Milwaukee, WI
(414) 354-8950

The Black Kettle Steakhouse since 1963 has had a reputation for consistent high quality food and service complimented by a beautiful unpretentious ambiance. Along with the best steaks in town, other entrees include - Baby Back B.B.Q. Ribs, Seafood, and Chicken Breast. Salads - Tenderloin Spinach with Blue Cheese, Sour Cream. Appetizers - our famous Onion Rings or Flaming "Jack" Cheese with homemade Croustines.

The featured recipe, Pepper Steak, is one that is both simple, unique and low fat with a very hardy flavor. It can be inter-changed with Grilled Chicken or Shrimp instead of sauteed tenderloin. You can also get more creative with different types of fresh vegetables. A Pinot Noire, Beaujolais, or even a Savignon Blanc would compliment this dish.

The Williamsburg charm of hardwood floors, stained glass windows, cozy fireplace or colorful Garden Room make for a romantic dinner or serious business luncheon. Forget stuffy reservations on Friday night Fish Frys or Saturday evenings, just come on in! Lunch served 11:30 - close, Monday - Friday. Dinners served 5:00 till close, Monday - Saturday. Closed Sunday except Mother's Day and Easter.

Grilled Atlantic Salmon

Remove pits from the Nicoise and dry-cured olives. Place on a cutting board with the anchovy, the garlic, and a few grinds of fresh black pepper from a pepper mill. Chop the ingredients together until they form a coarse paste. Place in a small mixing bowl and add 1 tablespoon of the olive oil, mix thoroughly. Taste and adjust seasoning if necessary, then let stand at room temperature 2 hours. Meanwhile, season the salmon steaks with salt and pepper, and rub them with 1 tablespoon of the olive oil. Prepare wood fire, grill or broiler. Combine remaining olive oil with the lemon juice in a small bowl, whisk together completely and season with salt and pepper. Pour into an old dressing bottle or an empty squeeze bottle. Prepare the salmon steaks to desired doneness (we like medium-rare). Set salmon steaks aside briefly in a warm place. Briefly grill the asparagus until heated through. Keep warm. Heat a small sauté pan over medium heat and add capers. Shake them around in the pan until well heated and they begin to pop, about 2 minutes. Remove from heat and add well shaken lemon dressing to the sauté pan. Taste and season. Divide the olive mixture between the four salmon steaks and spread over the top. Divide the warm lemon dressing between the four salmon steaks, and pour it over the top of the olive mixture. Serve immediately.

2 pounds Atlantic salmon fillet, skin & bones removed, divided into 4 equal pieces

8 ounces nicoise olives

4 ounces French oil-cured ripe olives

2 ounces capers (preferably non-pareils, very small), drained

1/2 anchovy filet

1/4 garlic clove

4 ounces extra virgin olive oil

1 ounce lemon juice

1 tablespoon sea salt

1 tablespoon black pepper, freshly ground

1 pound asparagus, peeled & blanched if large

The English Room

The English Room

The English Room
424 E. Wisconsin Ave.
Milwaukee, WI
(414) 273-8222

For a unique reflection of Milwaukee's history and some of the best dining in the city, visit The English Room at The Pfister Hotel. This award-winning restaurant began in 1926 as a small pub serving steaks and chops. During the 30's and 40's, The English Room became a popular gathering spot for prominent Milwaukeeans. Since 1962, The English Room has evolved into one of Milwaukee's finest restaurants and has been acclaimed both locally and nationally for its impeccable service and exceptional dining. Surrounded by selected pieces from The Pfister Hotel's collection of original 19th and early 20th century artwork, guests of The English Room will enjoy the culinary classics such as filet of beef, fresh salmon and roasted rack of lamb.

The atmosphere in The English Room truly defines elegance, making it the perfect setting for a pre-show meal or a late romantic dinner. Reservations are recommended and parking is available at The Pfister Hotel. The English Room serves Monday through Friday from 5:30 to 10:00 p.m., Saturdays from 5:30 to 11:00 p.m. and Sundays from 5:00 to 10 p.m.

Delicious combination of mushrooms and beef with a brandied flavored sauce.

Filet of Beef with Brandied Morel Mushroom Cream Sauce

Soak dry morels in water for 15 to 20 minutes or until soft. Season filets with salt and pepper. Heat olive oil in cast iron pan. Sauté filets to desired temperature and set aside. Add shallots (sauté until translucent) then add garlic into pan as well as the strained morels. Flame with brandy and reduce for 1 to 2 minutes. Add heavy cream and stir until consistency is creamy, reduce again, bind with brown sauce and add salt and pepper to taste. Once the desired consistency is reached, remove from heat and whip butter into sauce. Do not boil again. Serve with buttered egg noodles and vegetable of choice.

Serves 4.

4 8 ounce center cut filets of beef

salt and pepper

olive oil

1/2 quart heavy cream

20 to 30 pieces of dried morels

2 tablespoons finely chopped shallots

1/4 teaspoon fresh minced garlic

1/2 cup demi-glaze (substitute with a brown sauce)

dash of brandy

1 to 2 teaspoons of butter

Fox & Hounds

1298 Friess Lake Rd.
Hubertus, WI
(414) 251-4100

Nestled in Wisconsin's scenic Kettle Moraine, the Fox and Hounds Restaurant is the perfect setting for all occasions: a romantic fireside table for two, a gathering of friends or family, employee Christmas party, a rehearsal dinner or a grand scale wedding.

Our menu offers a wide variety of foods, aged beef, seafood and a selection of country oven dinners, including our signature "Roast Goose." To compliment our menu we offer a full service bar, including over 50 domestic and imported beers as well as an award winning wine list.

Reservations are always recommended and appreciated. Valet parking, handicap accessible. Closed Sundays and Mondays. Open 4:00pm daily and most holidays. Banquet facilities up to 150 people.

A delightful combination of cream and sherry to enhance the delicate veal medallions.

Veal Medallions Aux Sacher

Bring to a boil beef stock, beef base, onion powder, garlic powder, sweet leaf basil and dill weed. Add beef roux and stir until consistency of heavy cream. Reduce heat and simmer 20 to 30 minutes, removing foam. Adjust flavor with salt and pepper. Add half and half and remove from heat. Add the cream sherry. Makes about 5 cups of Sacher Sauce.

Use three of the 2 ounce medallions per person. Coat medallions with flour and pan fry in hot pan with butter. (Do not let butter burn.) Fry for about one and one-half minutes per side. Serve immediately.

Sacher Sauce

1 quart beef stock

1/4 cup beef base

1 tablespoon onion powder

1/2 teaspoon garlic powder

1/2 teaspoon sweet leaf basil

pinch dill weed

3/4 to 1 ounce beef roux

3/4 cup half and half

1/2 cup cream sherry

Veal Medallions

2 ounce veal medallions

flour

butter

Red Circle Inn
N44 W33013 Watertown Plank Rd.
Nashotah, WI
(414) 367-4883

Red Circle Inn

Celebrating 150 Years
1848-1998

The rich and colorful history of The Red Circle Inn dates back 150 years to 1848 when Francis Schraudenbach, a Bavarian immigrant, built a stagecoach stop that consisted of an inn with a tavern and dining room. Known as the Nashotah Inn, it was a stopover for traders, trappers and settlers looking for comfortable lodging and good food as they hauled their crops, furs and supplies over Watertown Plank Road. In 1854, the Chicago, Milwaukee, Watertown and Baraboo Valley Railroad was built through Nashotah, and due to its increased accessibility, The Lake Country Area became popular as a summer residence for the wealthy industrial and brewery families of Milwaukee.

The Inn changed owners several times until Captain Frederick Pabst and the Pabst Brewing Company purchased it in 1898 and changed the name to The Red Circle Inn, because a "red circle" was a famous part of the trademark label, and a symbol of quality. The Polaski family took over the Inn in 1911 and rebuilt the main building after a fire in 1917. The Red Circle Inn stayed in the Polaski family until 1976 when Provini Veal and its chairman Art Groenevelt bought the Inn.

Nico Derni and Norm Eckstaedt, also owners of The Elm Grove Inn, purchased The Red Circle Inn in 1993, and have ever since perpetuated and enhanced the restaurants long tradition of fine food and service. Serving the freshest of fish and hand cut steaks in unique "Country French" influenced cuisine, the Circle is rated as one of Wisconsin's finest.

... fine Wisconsin veal cooked in an old world European style with a country French influence.

Osso Bucco Cassoulet

Osso Bucco: Lightly flour and sauté veal shanks in clarified butter with 1 cup diced onion, 1 bay leaf, pinch of thyme, 1/4 cup of garlic, pepper and salt to taste. Sauté until light brown on both sides. Then add veal stock, 1/2 cup of white wine and 1 cup of tomatoes with their juice and skin, just to cover the meat. Cover with foil and bake in a 325 degree oven for 2 hours or until tender.

Cassoulet: Sauté bacon until fat has rendered, add remaining onion and garlic and sauté for 2 to 3 minutes and add 2 cups of diced tomatoes, beans, 1/2 cup of white wine and veal stock just to cover the beans and simmer for one and one-half hours at a slow boil or until tender.

Osso Bucco Cassoulet: Mix beans and veal and all stock together stirring to blend all flavors for 15 minutes and serve with toasted French bread lightly buttered and topped with parmesan cheese.

Serves 3 to 4 people.

6 pieces "cross cut" veal shank, 2 inches thick

clarified butter

flour

2 cups diced onions

1/2 cup minced garlic

3 cups skinless, seeded, diced tomatoes

tomato juice and skin

1 pound rinsed and soaked northern white beans

1/2 pound bacon

2 bay leaves

thyme

black pepper

salt

veal stock

1 cup white wine

Boder's on the River
11919 N. River Road
43W, Mequon, WI
(414) 242-0335

The place where people go to make special times more special. In 1929 its owners, John and Frieda Boder, decided to open Boder's Tea Room in Mequon. Milwaukeeans enjoyed the long drive to the country. They would spend the day at the beach on the river and enjoy lunch, dinner or afternoon tea. John and Frieda's son, Jack, and his wife, Dolly, bought the restaurant in 1954. Their muffins, fruit plate and fritters became the hallmark of Boder's signature dishes. Their children eventually took over and added other specialties which keep Boder's among Milwaukee's top 25 restaurants. Boder's is known for being the place to go to make special times even more special. As the fourth generation of family becomes involved with business, we will continue that tradition while adapting to your changing tastes. Our goal is to exceed the expectations of people who love to eat.

Stuffed Rainbow Trout

Break bread into small pieces in mixing bowl. Combine parsley, onion and salt. Mix with bread. Add milk, wine, melted butter and egg. Mix well with electric mixer on low speed. Do not over mix. Stuff trout with dressing. Flour trout lightly and sprinkle with salt, melted butter and paprika. Place trout on well buttered pan and bake at 400 degrees for about 20 minutes or until golden brown and fish is flaky. Serve with lemon and tartar sauce.

12 slices white bread

2 tablespoons chopped parsley

1 teaspoon grated onion

2 teaspoons salt

3/4 cup milk

1/3 cup dry sauterne wine

1/2 cup melted butter

1 egg

4 rainbow trout

flour

salt

1 tablespoon butter

paprika

Weissgerber's Gasthaus
2720 N. Grandview Blvd.
Waukesha, WI
(414) 544-4460

Three generations of the Weissgerber family have built and still operate the Gasthaus Inn Restaurant in Waukesha, perhaps the most authentic German Restaurant in Wisconsin. The Roast Goose - Watertown was originally conceived at the family's Seven Seas Restaurant and brought to the Gasthaus due to its unique German - Alsatian - Wisconsin character. The Roast Goose Watertown is so named because Watertown was once the goose capitol of America. The entree has its roots in the Alsace region near the border of France and Germany and is enhanced with a cranberry-cherry sauce, and wild rice grown by American Indians in Wisconsin.

Our family was honored to serve the Roast Goose - Watertown to President Bush in October of 1992 during his Whistle-Stop campaign trip through our state from Burlington to Chippewa Falls.

The Gasthaus Restaurant features a great selection of American as well as German entrées and outstanding Wine and Beer selections. The restaurant is open seven days a week for Dinner and Monday through Friday for Lunch.

*Roast Goose "Watertown"
- fit for the President!*

Roast Goose "Watertown"

Heat oven to 400 degrees. Season the four pieces of goose with salt and pepper. Brown in oven with vegetables until golden and remove. Set goose and vegetables in a deep pan and add stock to cover. For ease of preparation and imparting of good flavor, combine chicken and beef bouillon stock. Cover pan tightly with lid or aluminum foil and bake for 2 and one-half to 3 hours until tender. Meanwhile heat cranberries in water and wine until cranberries pop open. Turn down to simmer; add dry ingredients and stir for 1 minute. Then add cherries and marmalade and bring to light boil. Mix cold water and corn starch together and add to simmering sauce. Sauce should be at a light boil. Bring to a boil and remove. Serve hot with goose. When goose has finished cooking, remove the foil and crisp the outside of the goose meat to seal in its moisture and flavor. Serve traditional style with a sweet sauerkraut or seasonal with white and wild rice mix, baby potatoes or squash.

May we suggest an Alsatian Spatburgunder (Pinot Noir) or a Pinot Noir from California or France's Burgundy. A Beaujolais Nouveau or Beaujolais Villages would also work very nicely.

1 whole goose, quartered

1 onion, coarsely chopped

2 carrots, coarsely chopped

3 stalks celery, coarsely chopped

salt and pepper to taste

1 quart brown stock

1 cup fresh cranberries

1 cup tart cherries, pitted

one and one-half cups water

1/4 cup cabernet sauvignon

1/4 teaspoon ground ginger

1/4 teaspoon ground cinnamon

2 tablespoons sugar

1 tablespoon brown sugar

2 tablespoons apricot or peach marmalade

1 tablespoon cold water

1 tablespoon corn starch

26

MIMMAS
CAFE ®

Mimma's Cafe
1307 E. Brady St.
Milwaukee, WI
(414) 271-7337

Located in the newly revitalized and vibrant Brady Street area, Mimma's Cafe features the best of Italy in the heart of Milwaukee. Mimma's ever-changing menu boasts weekly regional specialties, over fifty varieties of pasta, as well as time honored chef's favorites... a distinctive difference in dining, all served with a unique flair discriminating diners have come to enjoy.

Whether it's business or pleasure, Mimma's Cafe is the perfect meeting place to savor world class Italian cuisine in a casual atmosphere. Some of Mimma's honors include: Milwaukee Magazine's Readers Choice Award and listed in Zagat's Top 1000 Restaurants in the U.S.A.

A flavorful blend of smoked salmon, farfalle pasta and roasted red bell peppers.

Farfalle Al Salmone Affumicato

(1) Roast the peppers under the broiler or over an open flame until the skin is charred on all sides. Place them in a bowl and cover the bowl tightly with plastic wrap. After about 20 minutes, take the peppers out, cut them in half, remove the core and scrape away the blistered skin and the seeds. Place the peppers and the garlic in a food processor or blender and grind until creamy. Remove and set aside.

(2) Bring 4 quarts of water to a boil in a large saucepan or pot, add 1 tablespoon of salt and drop in the pasta all at once, stirring well.

(3) Flake the smoked salmon with a fork. Put the fish, the pepper purée and the cream in a large skillet over a medium-high heat. Season with salt to taste (the salmon is already salty) and black pepper, and cook until the cream has reduced by half. Stir in the basil and remove from the heat.

(4) When the pasta is cooked al dente, drain it and toss it with the sauce. Serve at once.

Also good with Penne, Fusilli, or Conchiqlie.

2 red bell peppers

2 garlic cloves, peeled

1/2 pound flakeable smoked salmon

1 cup heavy cream

salt and freshly ground black pepper

2 tablespoons shredded fresh basil

1 pound of farfalle pasta

Mader's

Mader's German Restaurant
1037 N. Old World Third St.
Milwaukee, WI
(414) 271-3377

Experience all the flavor of Mader's great heritage of German specialties. Mader's offers specialties you'll find nowhere else. Try our oxtail or liver dumpling soup, the Kaiser's fresh spinach salad with hot bacon dressing, popendorf, Austria's sauerkraut balls or Germany's koenigth pastete. Mader's new private party facility, the Baron's Rhine Stube, accommodates up to 110 guests. The Rhine Stube features its own private bar. After dinner savor a sampling of Vienna's gift to the world: its renowned cakes and tortes, chocolate sacher torte or cherry filled black forest torte.

Duckling with a raspberry chambord sauce served with wild rice and pecans...

Duck Chambord

Place seasoned ducks on rack in roasting pan. Add water. Roast breast side up at 375 degrees for 1 1/2 hours and flip. Roast back side up for 1 hour and flip back. Roast about 1 1/4 hours until duck is tender. Remove ducks from pan and set aside until cooled. Save remaining drippings from pan and skim fat from top. This is your duck stock. Split ducks and debone by taking rib cage and wish bone out. Cut duck into four pieces and place in sauté pan. Top each piece with chambord glaze. Add whole raspberries as a garnish.

Chambord Raspberry Glaze: Melt butter and sugar in sauce pan until it reaches carmelization. Add hot duck stock and stir until dissolved. Add corn starch to medium thickness. Whip in raspberry jelly and remove from heat. Add chambord liqueur.

3 or 4 4 1/2 pound ducks

6 ounces seedless raspberry jam

3 ounces chambord liqueur

2 cups wild rice

raspberries for garnish

1/4 cup pecan pieces

1/3 cup sugar

1/4 cup diced onions

1/2 ounce butter

10 ounces duck stock

corn starch mixed with cold water for thickening

The Packing House

Packing House
900 E. Layton
Milwaukee, WI
(414) 483-5054

The Packing House was founded by the Wiken family in 1974 and is still owned and operated by them today. The menu has something for everyone's taste whether you join them for lunch, dinner, Friday Fish Fry or Sunday Brunch. The specialties include Steaks, like the award-winning Garlic Stuffed Filet (recipe here) and Steak au Poivre. You can also choose from many other varieties of entrees like their famous Bar-B-Que Ribs, many excellent Seafood dishes like Shrimp specialties, Lobster and many Fresh Fish selections. You will not be disappointed at The Packing House. Their attentive staff and inviting atmosphere will please the most discriminating diner. The Packing House also features live Jazz Wednesday through Saturday nights in their lounge.

This barrel-shaped filet is stuffed with garlic slivers, wrapped in bacon, seared and sealed. One of our most popular steaks, it won the Wisconsin State Fair's Best of Show. It is truly a beautiful presentation that will make your tastebuds sing.

Garlic Stuffed Filet with Dijon Mustard Sauce

Preheat oven to 400 degrees. Slice garlic as thin as possible, then slice again to create slivers. Using the clean pointed end of a skewer, poke five holes evenly spaced on end of filet. Push one garlic sliver into each hole. Turn filet over and do the same on the other end. Season filet with seasoning salt. Cross bacon strips on work table, place filet down directly over cross, bring up sides of bacon over lap and tuck under. (Best to do 4 hours in advance so garlic can permeate the steak.) Heat oil in frying pan medium high heat. Add filet over lapped and tucked side first. Fry until bacon is crisp. Carefully turn over and crisp other side. Take steak out, place into a pie pan and bake 10-15 minutes depending on your desired doneness. Use a meat thermometer 140 for medium.

For Dijon Mustard Sauce:

Mix first 7 ingredients in a medium saucepan, bring to simmer over medium heat, reducing by 1/4. Mix cornstarch and water in a separate bowl, stir into simmering sauce to thicken. Add butter 1 piece at a time, mixing constantly. Yields 1 cup.

Filet

1 10 ounce center cut beef tender filet

1 clove garlic

2 strips bacon

seasoning salt

2 tablespoons oil

Dijon Mustard Sauce

8 ounces chicken stock

2 tablespoons Dijon mustard

2 tablespoons dry vermouth

1/2 teaspoon cracked black pepper

1 teaspoon parsley flakes

1 teaspoon sugar

1/4 teaspoon salt

1/4 pound unsalted butter (cut into small pieces)

2 teaspoons cornstarch

2 teaspoons water

Jack Pandl's Whitefish Bay Inn

WHITEFISH BAY
Since 1915
Inn

Jack Pandl's Whitefish Bay Inn
1319 E. Henry Clay St.
Milwaukee, WI
(414) 964-3800

Jack Pandl's Whitefish Bay Inn, one of the area's oldest restaurants, is celebrating over 82 years at the same location and under the same ownership of the same family. Designated a Milwaukee County landmark, the building is basically unchanged from the way it appeared in 1915, reminiscent of the unhurried past. Inside, one of the Midwest's largest and finest collections of antique beer steins is on display. We are well known for our broiled whitefish (hand boned and always fresh). The German pancake unique to Jack Pandl's is served at brunch, lunch, dinner or for dessert. Soups and desserts are prepared from scratch. In addition to our menu, creative specials are served daily. Reservations are recommended during weekends and holidays. Open 7 days a week, we offer all menu items for take-out or delivery. With a friendly atmosphere of hospitality and warmth, you are a stranger here but once.

A light, flaky, flavorful fish perfect for the health conscious diner.

Fresh Broiled Whitefish

To debone whitefish fillets, spread fillets skin-side-down on a cutting board. Gently brush fillets from head to tail with fingers to raise the bones. Using sanitized needle nose pliers, pull the bones while holding down the flesh on either side of the pliers nose so as not to remove any flesh.

Line a baking sheet with foil. Place the fillets skin-side-down on the sheet and lightly brush with oil. Lightly salt. Broil the filets 8 to 10 minutes or until the fish is flaky, but not dry. Re-oiling may be necessary after 4 or 5 minutes. Flesh should turn white and begin separating when done. Sprinkle lightly with paprika and cook another minute. Carefully remove from the baking sheet so that the skin is left stuck to the foil. Place on warm plates and garnish with lemon wedge and parsley sprig.

Take care not to over cook the fish.

vegetable oil

6 8 ounce whitefish fillets

paprika

6 lemon wedges

6 parsley sprigs

salt

34

Heaven City Restaurant
S91 W27850 Hwy. ES
Mukwonago, WI
(414) 363-5191

Heaven City. The name conjures images of clouds, harps and angels. But the award-winning Waukesha County restaurant that proudly carries the name has had a checkered past. Its colorful history includes being a religious commune (hence the name) but its short stint as a house of, ahem, dubious morals was probably more interesting. That brief fall from grace has long since been absolved. Heaven City is now considered by food critics to be among the best restaurants in south-eastern Wisconsin. Now an important part of the community's restaurant scene, Heaven City specializes in contemporary midwestern cuisine, where chef Scott McGlinchey and his wife Mandy, now sole owners of the restaurant have hands on in all creations in the kitchen. McGlinchey emphasizes use of fresh ingredients which he purchases from local farmers. With these ingredients Chef McGlinchey features special menus as well as the house menu. The restaurant is striving to become a leader in southeastern Wisconsin for its variety and creative approach in food presentation. It has already won numerous awards and has been judged one of the 25 best restaurants in the state.

...with exotic mushroom risotto and Wollersheim Domaine du Sac balsamic butter sauce.

Whitewater Salmon

Risotto- Sauté onion and garlic in olive oil over medium heat until onion is translucent. Add Aborio rice. Slowly add chicken stock mixed with the mushroom powder and caramel color, approximately 1/3 cup at a time stirring constantly. Add sautéed mushrooms with the last 1/3 cup of stock. Spread out and cool on sheet pan and set aside. When ready to serve, place risotto in large sauté pan over medium heat. Add stock and cook. When it starts to dry up, add butter, cream and lastly, pecorino cheese. Remove from heat.

Salmon- Season salmon fillets with seasoning mix, (coriander, salt & pepper). Heat pan over high heat. Add oil and sear fillets, approximately 2 minutes on each side and remove from pan. Plate risotto and place salmon on top.

Sauce- In pan fish was cooked in, add 4 tablespoons of butter and brown. Add Wollersheim Domaine du Sac, balsamic vinegar and salt & pepper. Pour around risotto.

Spinach- Flash fry spinach in hot oil and garnish top of salmon.

Enjoy with the rest of your Wollersheim Domaine du Sac!

4 ounces diced onion

1 teaspoon chopped garlic

2 ounces olive oil

1 cup Aborio rice

2 cups chicken stock and beef stock blended (or 1 bouillon cube of each)

1 teaspoon mushroom powder

1 teaspoon caramel color

1 cup exotic mushrooms, sliced and sautéed

12 ounces stock

3 ounces cream

2 tablespoons raw butter

4 tablespoons pecorino cheese

4 salmon fillets

coriander, salt & pepper mix (equal parts)

1 tablespoon oil

4 tablespoons raw butter

2 ounces Wollersheim Domaine du Sac wine

2 ounces balsamic vinegar

1/2 bag spinach, picked and cleaned

6 ounces oil

Elm Grove Inn
13275 Watertown Plank Rd.
Elm Grove, WI
(414) 782-7090

The Elm Grove Inn, built in 1855 by the Reusch family, is the second oldest operating restaurant in Wisconsin. Serving the community not only as an Inn offering food and lodging, in the past, the building also housed a General Store, Post Office, and an adjoining building with a livery stable and blacksmith's shop.

Remaining in the Reusch family until the late 1950s, numerous successful operators ran the restaurant. In 1989, current owners Nico Derni, born in the Provence region of France, and Norm Eckstaedt, a native of Milwaukee, have renovated and established the Inn as one of the area's finest dining destinations. They also own The Red Circle Inn in Nashotah, Wisconsin, which will celebrate its 150th anniversary in 1998.

Local restaurant critics have given consistently high marks to the service and French-influenced cuisine. Only top-quality fresh foods and spirits grace the tables of the Inn with its comfortable, warm Williamsburg motif.

Delicate pike from fresh Wisconsin waters baked to enhance its fresh, sweet flavor.

Fresh Walleye Pike En Papillotie

Cut parchment paper into a heart shape. In center of paper place vegetables topped with pike fillet. Place a pinch of dill, salt and pepper and pat of butter atop fish and dash of wine. Butter the face of the parchment and seal fish inside by folding and crimping the edge.

Bake in a 375 degree oven for 10 minutes or until parchment "balloons" and is golden.

Serve in parchment with drawn butter and fresh dill on the side with steamed root vegetables of carrot, new potato and pearl onion on the side.

Serves 1.

10 to 12 ounces skinless filleted walleye pike

julienned carrot, celery and leek (3 to 4 pieces of each)

salt and pepper

fresh dill

1/2 ounce white wine

1 pat sweet butter

2 ounces clarified butter

15 inch by 15 inch parchment paper

Chip & Py's
1340 W. Towne Square Rd.
Mequon, WI
(414) 241-9589

Chip & Py's is a uniquely innovative, sophisticated restaurant with a relaxing, contemporary atmosphere. You can always enjoy the smooth sounds of jazz. On Wednesday, Friday and Saturday evenings live jazz ensembles feature favorite local piano talents. Chip & Py's extensive jazz CD collection fills in throughout the week.

Chip & Py's comfortable bar area caters to almost every taste. The wine list includes domestic favorites as well as an excellent selection of imported labels. You will be delighted with the extensive list of wines by the glass.

A tempting selection of mouth-watering cuisine includes Salmon with Sesame Plum Sauce, Tuscan Chicken, Vegetarian Fettuccine and Steak au Poivre. We also offer lighter meals such as Herb Chicken Sandwich, Caesar Salad (with or without Shrimp or Chicken), Spinach Pie, Porcini Mushroom Pasta or a Sicilian Steak Sandwich. Patio dining available in summer.

Chip & Py's - Where fun people have a great time.

Salmon with Sesame Plum Sauce

Mix sesame oil, red pepper, ginger and garlic. Heat until soft. Add remaining ingredients, whisk and keep warm. Coat salmon fillets lightly with vegetable oil and either grill or broil for 2 to 3 minutes on each side until done. Top with 2 ounces sauce and serve with rice pilaf and steamed broccoli.

5 tablespoons sesame oil

1/2 teaspoon flaked red pepper

1 tablespoon minced ginger

1 1/2 large garlic cloves, minced

3/4 cup plum sauce

5 tablespoons balsamic vinegar

5 tablespoons soy sauce

5 tablespoons fresh orange juice

2 1/2 teaspoons ground coriander

1 1/4 teaspoons Chinese 5 spice

8 7 to 9 ounce salmon fillets

vegetable oil

Albanese's Roadhouse

Albanese's Roadhouse
2301 Bluemound Rd.
Waukesha, WI
(414) 785-1930

Experience the fine casual dining experience that Southeastern Wisconsin residents have enjoyed for more than 54 years. Albanese's is a family-owned restaurant, specializing in homemade Italian dishes. The specialties include, Albanese's famous angel hair pasta, as well as the popular Friday night fish fry. Although Albanese's specializes in traditional Italian pastas; entrees also include, seafood, chicken, pizza, veal and beef dinners. Dinner served Monday through Thursday, 5 to 10p.m., Friday and Saturday, 5 to 11p.m. and Sunday 4:30 to 9p.m. Lunch Friday only 11:30a.m. to 2p.m. Cocktail hour Monday through Thursday, 4 to 6p.m. Albanese's accepts reservations for parties of seven or more.

Italian Sausage Cacciatore

While browning Italian sausages in pan, julienne onion and peppers. Slice mushrooms. Sauté garlic lightly in 2 tablespoons olive oil. Add peppers, mushrooms and onions and continue sautéing until onions appear clear. Add wine, rosemary, tomatoes and sauce. Lower heat and simmer. Slice Italian sausage into bite size pieces, add to mixture. Simmer for 10 minutes.

5 regular or hot Italian sausages

1/2 tablespoon chopped garlic

1/2 small onion, julienned

1 medium green pepper, julienned

1 medium red pepper

4 to 8 ounces mushrooms

1/8 cup marsala wine

1 can diced tomatoes

3/4 teaspoon rosemary

2 cups pasta sauce

Eagan's
1030 N. Water St.
Milwaukee, WI
(414) 271-6900

Located in the heart of Milwaukee's bustling entertainment district, Eagan's is synonymous with fresh, tantalizing seafood. A wide variety of oysters grace the most extensive raw bar in the city; just one facet of the classic culinary experience that awaits you. Elegant, cosmopolitan, and adorned with beautiful French impressionist murals, Eagan's is the heart and soul of the vibrant nightlife scene.

The pepper seared ahi is normally served as an appetizer at Eagan's. Because of its popularity, however, many customers order it as an entree-sized portion. Most customers feel it is best when the tuna, avocado, ginger, and Wasabi sauce are all consumed together. Use the highest grade tuna that you can find and remember that it is best when prepared rare to medium rare.

A wonderfully unique Japanese-style way of preparing fresh tuna.

Pepper Seared Ahi Tuna

For the Wasabi sauce, mix the mustard, mayonnaise and Wasabi paste together and chill (hold in a plastic squirt bottle if possible.) To prepare the tuna, mix the peppercorns and the breadcrumbs together. Lightly coat an 8 ounce piece of tuna with sesame oil, then cover it with the peppercorn mixture. Make sure it is coated well. Place a sauté pan on high heat. Coat the bottom of the pan with sesame oil. Sauté the tuna for three minutes on each side. On the plate, make a cross-hatched pattern with the Wasabi sauce on the plate. (If you do not have a squirt bottle, just spread the sauce on the bottom of the plate.) Cut the tuna in half and place the pieces on the bottom-center of the plate. Cut the avocado into a fan and place it just above the tuna, and form the ginger into a small rose and place it next to the avocado. Cilantro can be used as a garnish for the plate.

2 ounces Dijon mustard

2 ounces mayo

1/2 teaspoon Wasabi paste

8 ounce portions of tuna cut into triangles

salt as needed

1/2 cup dry bread crumbs

1/4 cup cracked black peppercorns

sesame oil as needed

1/4 avocado

pickled ginger

cilantro leaves

2-3 ounces Wasabi sauce

44

Crawdaddy's
6414 W. Greenfield
West Allis, WI
(414) 778-2228

Centrally located in the city of West Allis, Crawdaddy's proves to be a true "diamond in the rough." Open for over two-and-a-half years, it remains among the metro area's hottest new restaurants. Crawdaddy's consistently draws patrons from as far as Chicago for what Chef/Owner Jonathan Klug refers to as his 'own unique style of seafood-driven Cajun Fusion cuisine.' The atmosphere at Crawdaddy's is casual yet lively, featuring the best of Cajun Zydeco and Blues music and an extensive array of Louisiana artwork. Coupled with the traditional New Orleans specialties on the regular menu is an extensive and ever-changing nightly special menu, incorporating elements found in various other cuisines with exciting flair. An old favorite on the menu at Crawdaddy's, this dish can easily be reproduced at home with great results.

A beautiful presentation with fresh vegetables and wild rice.

Lacquered Boudin-Stuffed Quail

For the quail, preheat the oven to 350 degrees. Remove the boudin sausage from its casings and use it to stuff the quail. Lightly season the quail with salt, pepper and Cajun seasoning. Bake the quail at 300 degrees for 40-45 minutes on a greased sheet pan.

For the sauce, combine the port wine, sherry, sugar and balsamic vinegar together in a heavy-bottomed saucepan and slowly reduce the mixture over low heat until it resembles syrup in texture. Remove the reduction from the stove and whisk in the butter until all of it has been incorporated.

*Boudin sausage is available at Rushing Waters Trout Farm in Palmyra, WI.

Ingredients for the Quail

8 4 ounce Manchester Farm's semi-boneless European-style quail

2 pounds Thibodeaux's rice and pork boudin-sausage

salt and pepper

Cajun seasoning

Ingredients for the Sauce

2 cups ruby port wine

1 cup sherry

1 teaspoon sugar

2 tablespoons balsamic vinegar

1/2 pound unsalted butter, cut into small pieces

46

the Anchorage

Anchorage Restaurant
4700 N. Pt. Washington Rd.
Milwaukee, WI
(414) 962-4710

The Anchorage Restaurant has set the standard for fine seafood dining in Milwaukee for the past 23 years. Its warmth, elegance and charm are highlighted with a beautiful view of the wooded banks of the Milwaukee River. The Anchorage specializes in fresh seafood flown in from all three coasts. New menu items are constantly being developed and introduced as daily "specials". Standard menu items such as The Anchorage Scallops and the Red Snapper Soup are favorites of Restaurant Critics around the city. For outdoor dining, the Anchorage Patio is serene and relaxing — weather permitting — it is a must!

Fresh walleye pike coated in a Dijon pecan miede pain, pan fried, and finished with a Dijon chive beurre blanc.

Fresh Walleye Pike

Dredge walleye fillets in flour, coating both sides. Combine Dijon mustard and white wine. Brush the meat side of the walleye with this mixture until fully coated. In shallow bowl, combine Japanese bread crumbs, ground up pecans, and 3 pinches of white pepper. Press the coated side of the walleye into this mixture. Brown fish in the olive oil until tender. Top with Dijon-chive beurre blanc.

4 walleye pike fillets

flour

4 tablespoons Dijon mustard

4 tablespoons white wine

Japanese bread crumbs

ground pecans

white pepper

1/2 cup olive oil

Sauce

1 cup white wine

1/2 quart heavy cream

1/2 cup diced onions

1 tablespoon whole peppercorns

1/4 pound raw butter

1 teaspoon Dijon mustard

chopped chives

Toy's Chinatown Restaurant
830 N. 3rd St.
Milwaukee, WI
(414) 271-5166

TOY'S
Chinatown Restaurant

Welcome to Toy's Chinatown Restaurant, the oldest Chinese restaurant in Milwaukee since 1912. For an unforgettable dining experience, enjoy our superior Chinese cooking as you watch professional chefs masterfully prepare traditional dishes from our magnificent viewing kitchen. We take pride in preparing each entrée with an artistic flair only found at Toy's. Located on Old World Third Street across from the Hyatt downtown. Lunch and dinner served, call for reservations.

Seafood in Bird's Nest

Marinate scallops and shrimp in a dash of salt, dash of sugar, 1 teaspoon cooking sherry and a dash of fresh ginger. Marinate for 15 minutes, turning occasionally. Heat wok and add 1 teaspoon of oil. Add the marinade mixture and cook for about 1 minute in a very hot wok until shrimp and scallops are done (white in appearance). Take from wok and set aside. Heat wok. Add 1 teaspoon of oil and brown garlic. Add vegetable mixture. Stir fry for 1 minute, add seafood mixture and crab meat. Stir fry with 2 ounces of chicken broth. Add dash of salt, dash of white pepper, splash of sesame seed oil and 1 tablespoon of cornstarch. Finish cooking for 1 minute. Serve on a bed of rice noodles or with white rice.

4 jumbo shrimp

5 jumbo scallops

2 ounces crab meat

1/2 teaspoon salt

dash of sugar

1 teaspoon cooking sherry

dash of fresh ginger

2 ounces chicken broth

splash of sesame seed oil

1/2 clove garlic

2 teaspoons oil

dash of white pepper

1 tablespoon cornstarch

<u>8 ounces of Vegetable Mix</u>

canned baby corn

fresh broccoli

fresh mushrooms

fresh snow peas

straw mushrooms

sliced carrots

Aliota's

ON THE BLUEMOUND

Aliota's on Bluemound
19165 W. Bluemound Rd.
Brookfield, WI
(414) 782-4551

For over 46 years, Aliota's on Bluemound has been a restaurant experienced in excellence and tradition. From its continental cuisine featuring Sicilian dishes, steaks, chops, pasta and seafood served in a warm and friendly atmosphere, along with live entertainment in our lounge 6 nights a week, Aliota's offers a full dining experience. In addition to regular dining, the restaurant has party facilities for up to 65 people for that special occasion. The featured recipe, veal scallopine ala Aliota, promotes the use of fresh vegetables in a spicy tomato sauce along with medallions of prime veal steak. Served with an Italian salad, a cup of Minestrone soup (famous all over Milwaukee), a side of pasta with marinara sauce and a full bodied red wine, this dish will please even the most discriminating diner.

A savory blend of veal, fresh vegetables and a spicy tomato sauce, this dish goes well with other meats.

Veal Scallopine a la Aliota

In a medium saucepan over medium heat, melt 6 ounces of butter or margarine, and sauté green peppers and mushrooms about five minutes. Add diced tomatoes and seasonings and bring mixture to boil. Combine corn starch and water into a slur, and thicken mixture to a gravy-like consistency. Add the Romano cheese and blend well. Set aside. In a large skillet, melt rest of butter or margarine over medium heat and after dusting veal medallions in flour, sauté until golden brown on both sides. Place in a 9 x 11 baking dish and cover with sauce. Place in a preheated 350 degree oven and bake for 10 minutes or until sauce is hot.

12 2 ounce sliced veal steak medallions

1 cup flour

1/2 pound butter or margarine

1 large green pepper chopped in 1/2 inch pieces

1 pound fresh sliced mushrooms

14-1/2 ounce can of diced tomatoes

1 tablespoon granulated garlic

1 tablespoon salt

1 teaspoon pepper

2 tablespoons dry whole sweet basil

2 tablespoons grated romano cheese

2 tablespoons corn starch

1 cup water

52

Harold's

Harold's
4747 S. Howell Ave.
Milwaukee, WI
(414) 481-8000

Harold's Restaurant is setting up your perfect evening with quiet elegance, award winning cuisine and wines of distinction.

Chef Axel Dietrich enhances the traditional favorites with accents from around the world. One such featured recipe, "Seafood Mediterranean", blends the treasures of the sea in a delicate cream sauce - truly an Epicurean delight! We also offer delicious desserts to highlight your dining enjoyment.

Harold's is open for lunch and dinner Monday through Friday 11a.m. until 2 p.m., and 5 p.m. until 10 p.m. Saturday 5 p.m. until 11p.m. Closed Sundays.

Seafood Mediterranean

Pour olive oil in heated pan. Add shallots and garlic without browning. Immediately mix in all the seafood. Next, add tomatoes, lobster base, pesto, apricots and olives. Season to taste. Pour in the wine and let reduce to one half. Finally, add heavy cream and let reduce to proper thickness. Serve over fresh pasta. Serves 4-5 people.

2 ounces olive oil

4 teaspoons diced shallots

4 teaspoons crushed garlic

4 tablespoons sundried tomatoes (finely chopped)

2 teaspoons lobster base

2 teaspoons pesto

4 ounces dried apricots (slivered)

2 dozen stuffed green olives

16 large scallops

8 black mussels (cleaned & brushed)

8 raw large shrimp (peeled & deveined)

8 ounces lobster meat

8 cherry stone clams (cleaned & brushed)

salt & pepper to taste

4 ounces dry sherry

2 ounces Chablis

2 cups heavy cream

The King & I Restaurant
823 N. 2nd St.
Milwaukee, WI
(414) 276-4181

Experience the tantalizing entrees and authentic decor of Thailand at the King & I. The award winning restaurant features a variety of beef, chicken and seafood creations that have won the restaurant praise from local critics over the years. This restaurant also offers a daily lunch buffet giving all a chance to sample a variety of house specialties. Shrimp Pud Thai is one of Thailand's best known noodle dishes. It is eaten as a light meal. The King & I is located downtown.

A dish well balanced between spiciness and a sweet & sour taste.

Pud Thai

Soak rice noodles in warm water for 20 minutes, drain and set aside. Heat cooking pan over high heat and add vegetable oil.

Stir fry:

shrimp and garlic for 1 minute. Add egg; stir fry for 2 minutes then add noodles and half of the bean sprouts, ketchup, sugar, peanuts, fish sauce and dried red chili. Stir and turn for 2 minutes, add green onion, mix well. Remove to serving plate, garnish with Chinese parsley, bean sprouts and squeeze lime over noodles for sour taste.

1/2 pound rice noodles

5 medium shrimp (shelled & deveined)

2 eggs lightly beaten

3 garlic cloves finely chopped

1/2 pound bean sprouts

1 teaspoon sugar

1 tablespoon ketchup

1/4 cup ground roasted peanuts

1 tablespoon fish sauce

1 ounce green onion (cut into 2 inch lengths)

1 teaspoon dried red chili

1/4 cup vegetable oil

1/2 lime (quartered)

1/2 cup Chinese parsley

56

![Third Street Pier logo]

Third Street Pier
1110 N. Old World Third St.
Milwaukee, WI
(414) 272-0330

This culinary extravaganza is the creation of Friedrich von Holstein, director of Secret Service at the Prussian Court - a very reclusive but most powerful Politician under German Emperor Wilhelm I at the end of the 19th Century. Von Holstein was a connoisseur of food and wine. This entrée is representative of Milwaukee's hearty German cuisine because it combines some of the best food from land and water, making it a perfect presentation at our family's restaurant in the heart of Milwaukee's Downtown "by the river."

The Third Street Pier is one of the most romantic restaurants in Milwaukee with spectacular views of Milwaukee's skyline and the new pedestrian bridge linking eastern and western shores of the Milwaukee river. Diners enjoy watching the arrivals and departures of the Edelweiss Cruise Dining Boats catered by The Third Street Pier Restaurant. The menu combines some of the best entrées from the Weissgerber family restaurants and is complemented by an Award Winning Wine List. The restaurant is open seven days a week for lunch and dinner.

A classical German dish combining great food from land and water.

Schnitzel A La Holstein

Heat clarified butter, margarine or oil in frying pan. Pound cutlets with meat mallet to 1/4 inch thickness. In pie plate or flat bowl beat 4 additional eggs with salt and pepper. Coat veal in flour then dip in eggs, then coat with bread crumbs on both sides and put into pan. Brown the veal, but it should remain pink inside. Place cutlets on a heated dinner plate. Fry the four eggs sunny-side up and place on top of cutlets. Garnish the top of the eggs with anchovies and capers. Cut toasted bread into triangles and spread with butter. Decorate the toast points with sardines, smoked salmon and caviar and place on the platter with pickles to garnish. Serve with pan-fried potatoes.

May we suggest a heavier German white wine from the Paletinate (Pfalz) or a buttery Chardonnay from Southern California.

8 2 1/2 ounce veal cutlets

4 eggs

1/2 cup flour

1 cup dried bread crumbs

1/2 cup clarified butter or margarine

4 slices white toast

4 sardines in oil

4 anchovies

4 slices smoked salmon

4 small whole pickles

2 ounces caviar

58

Wildflowers

Located in the

Country Inn Hotel
& CONFERENCE CENTER

Wildflowers
2810 Golf Rd. (In The Country Inn Hotel)
Waukesha, WI
(414) 547-0201

We invite you to experience Wildflowers -- the signature restaurant of the Country Inn Hotel. The finest food and service that has earned the Country Inn Hotel its outstanding reputation is also the hallmark of Wildflowers.

Wildflowers is the showcase for the talents of the Country Inn Hotel's award-winning Certified Executive Chef David Davidson. Chef David is the 1997 American Culinary Federation Chef of the Year and the recipient of the Wisconsin Restaurants Association's Salute to Excellence Award. He has designed Wildflowers' menu for all tastes and all seasons and has created entrees like our featured Chicken Breast Dijon that will meet your highest expectations.

Weekends in Wildflowers feature our popular Friday Fish Fry, Sunday Breakfast Buffet and Sunday Prime Rib Buffet. From intimate dinners for two to small parties for those special occasions, we welcome you to "Experience the Difference" at Wildflowers Restaurant.

A Wildflowers favorite: a simple, yet elegant twist on a classic.

Chicken Breasts Dijon

For Dijon mayonnaise:

Mix together 2/3 cup mayonnaise, 1/3 cup Dijon mustard and 1 teaspoon dry mustard.

For bread crumbs:

Cut crusts off of white bread. Whip bread in mixer until fine.

Method:

Preheat oven to 325 degrees. Spray or butter 9 by 13 oven proof dish. Spread Dijon blend on top and bottom of each chicken breast, using all of the mixture. Lay breasts in baking dish and sprinkle bread crumbs over breasts. Bake until crumbs brown; about 18 to 22 minutes depending on oven. Meanwhile saute mushrooms and shallots in butter over medium heat; about 5 minutes. Add wine and cream. Reduce mixture about 10 minutes until thickened and coats the back of a spoon. Spoon mixture on warm plates and place breasts on top. Serve with fresh broccoli flowerettes.

4 6 ounce boneless, skinless chicken breasts

1 cup Dijon mayonnaise

1 cup white bread crumbs

2 tablespoons diced shallots

8 ounces sliced mushrooms

8 ounces Chardonnay

1 tablespoon butter

4 ounces cream

Salt and pepper

Seven Seas
1807 Nagawicka Rd.
Hartland, WI
(414) 367-3903

Bouillabaisse is a classical "all-purpose" fish meal originated by fishermen families around the Mediterranean and made most famous by seaside Restaurants of Marseilles. Its popularity has spread across the "Seven Seas" where our Restaurant prides itself of using the best ingredients and flavors with a hot touch of the pirates' spices. As the list of ingredients reflects, many varieties of shell and firm-fleshed fish from warm and cold waters are suitable for this very unique complete meal for the seafood lover. The Seven Seas Restaurant's recipe includes a wide band homemade pasta, a tradition very popular with fish soups along the Danube river of the old Austrian-Hungarian empire.

Our Seven Seas features great seafood and all-American Dinner recommendations with an award winning wine list. The Restaurant is open seven days a week for Dinner from May to October, and closed Tuesdays from November to April, and serves a wonderful Champagne Brunch on Sundays.

...a unique blend of slightly spicy seafood simmered in its own juices served over wide band pasta.

Bouillabaisse a la Seven Seas

Heat olive oil in deep, large saucepan and sauté onions, celery, carrots and garlic. Add tomatoes including juice, white wine, lemon juice, and remaining spices. Stir and add 12 cups of water. Adjust seasoning to taste, adding salt as needed. Cover, bring to a boil, and simmer for 10 minutes. Add cubed potatoes and simmer 15 minutes more. Add only the prepared shellfish to broth and simmer for 5 minutes. Add lobster and fish, cut into bite-size pieces with heads, bones and skin removed, simmer 5 minutes then add shrimp and simmer 7-10 minutes more or until seafood is done. Spoon separately cooked pasta into individual serving dishes and cover with 2 ladles of bouillabaisse, being sure to include a variety of seafood in each serving. Serve with salad and freshly baked garlic bread.

May we suggest a California Chardonnay or a dry Gewurtztraminer from Alsace or California as your wine selection to complement this unique and multi-flavored sailor's delicacy.

6 cherry stone clams
12 small clams
12 mussels
4 crab legs (split)
3 small lobster tails
(cut in half)
12 medium shrimp
2 firm fleshed fish - 1 pound
total
2 medium onions - chopped
2 cloves garlic
1 stalk celery
1 carrot
6 ounces white wine
2 tablespoons lemon juice
1 piece dried orange rind
2 potatoes -cubed/diced
5 ounces clam base
2 tablespoons chicken base
2 tablespoons basil
1 tablespoon marjoram
1 teaspoon cayenne pepper
1 tablespoon oregano
1/4 teaspoon Tabasco sauce
pinch of saffron
16 ounces can crushed
tomatoes
1 pound white band linguini
(or similar pasta)
1/2 cup olive oil

Welcome to

Saxe's
CASUAL FINE DINING

Established in 1985

Saxe's
1/4 mile west of Hwy. 83
on Hwy. 18
Genesee, WI
(414) 968-4600

Since opening in 1985, Tom and Lynn Saxe have continued to focus on the changing needs of their diverse clientele. They've brought a full-service dining and entertainment center to the rolling Kettle Moraine countryside that has become a popular gathering place for people of all ages. Where else can you find fine dining and casual dress mixed with televised sports in the bar and live entertainment in the lounge? Saxe's offers creative cuisine and freshly baked breads. Specials change daily and are consistently wonderful. Affordable country elegance abounds in our private banquet facility, accommodating up to 350 persons. Take a Sunday drive for our fabulous breakfast buffet served from 9:30 a.m. to 1 p.m. We are 3 minutes from Interstate 94, 7 minutes from Waukesha, 20 minutes from Brookfield Square. Just before the meadow and the woods.

Marinated herb chicken and pasta at its best.

Chicken and Tomato Basil Pasta

Marinate chicken in garlic and Italian herbs. Cut chicken into 1/2 to 3/4 ounce pieces and sauté in butter until 80 percent cooked. Add mushrooms. Deglaze with white wine and reduce. Add white sauce. Warm pasta in water bath. Toss in pasta and scallions. Serve in pasta bowl. Garnish with fresh parmesan and roma tomatoes.

12 ounce boneless skinless chicken breast

4 ounces white wine

8 ounces white sauce

3 ounces sliced mushrooms

1 ounce scallions

14 ounces tomato basil fettuccini

2 tablespoons butter

1 roma tomato

2 teaspoons fresh grated parmesan

2 teaspoons garlic

1 teaspoon Italian herbs

2 tablespoons olive oil

BARTH'S
...at the bridge

Barth's At The Bridge
N58 W6194 Columbia
Cedarburg, WI
(414) 377-0660

Nestled in the heart of historic Cedarburg on the banks of scenic Cedar Creek, you'll find a dining experience that's a feast for the eye and the appetite, featuring everything from good old-fashioned favorites to gourmet cuisine, fine wines and excellent cocktails.

The following recipe, Jäger Schnitzel, is an adaptation of a dish discovered by Chef Bruce Klug while dining in the biergarten of a local brewery in Heimenkirch, Germany.

Barth's is a palate pleaser the whole family will enjoy. The cozy candlelit dining rooms and cocktail lounge, lovely antique clocks and fine art—plus the courteous, friendly service—will make your visit to Barth's one that you'll want to repeat often. Reservations suggested. Lunch, dinner, Sunday brunch. Closed Monday.

Boneless pork loin with mushrooms, onions and bacon in a rich hunter style sauce.

Jäger Schnitzel

Heat sauce, tomato purée, tarragon and parsley in saucepan over low heat.

In a skillet, fry bacon until crisp. Remove crisp bacon, add to sauce. Drain all but 1 to 2 tablespoons bacon drippings from skillet. Sauté mushrooms and onions in drippings over medium-high heat until they begin to soften. Add wine to skillet and reduce by half. Add vegetable mixture to sauce.

Pound pork slices to 1/4" thickness and coat with flour. In a clean skillet, heat butter over medium high heat. Sauté pork slices until no longer pink, about 3 minutes on each side, adding more butter if needed.

Arrange pork slices on plate. Stir sour cream into sauce and ladle over meat.

Serves 4.

2 cups brown sauce
or demi-glace

1/4 cup tomato purée

1/2 teaspoon dried tarragon

2 teaspoons chopped
fresh parsley

1/4 pound raw bacon, diced

1/4 pound fresh mushrooms,
sliced, about 1 cup

1 small onion, julienned

1/4 cup dry white wine

8 slices boneless pork loin,
about 1 1/2 pounds

flour

2 tablespoons clarified
butter

2 tablespoons sour cream,
optional

Bavarian Wurst Haus

8310 W. Appleton Ave.
Milwaukee, WI
(414) 464-0060

The Bavarian Wurst Haus is where your Teutonic appetite can be catered to with Old World recipes and charm. Chef Norbert Holland tantalizes the taste buds of countless diners each year with the products of forty years of culinary experience and hopes your visit with us will be no exception. The Bavarian Wurst Haus is widely known for the variety and quality of its Bavarian cuisine with entrees such as our schnitzels and sausages, as well as many American offerings.

To match its cuisine, the Wurst Haus offers an authentic "Gasthaus" decor to make your dining experience even more unique. We know you will enjoy all of the sausage dishes, as seventy-five varieties are made with the highest of quality control in the Bavarian Wurst Haus' own sausage kitchen. You will find these excellent sausages available to take home in our adjacent Bavarian Sausage Mart. Contact Chef Norbert in advance and he will prepare your wild game for you and your guests.

For reservations call (414) 464-0060.

Braised Shank of Veal

(Shin of veal can be left whole or cut in 6 portions with bone removed.)

Heat fat in heavy skillet, rub salt over meat and brown on all sides. Add stock and white wine, onion, parsley root, bay leaf, cloves, thyme and pepper. Cover tightly and allow to sautée slowly, stirring from time to time. As the stock evaporates, use additional stock or water.

When meat is nearly tender, heat butter in skillet. Sautée vegetables; add salt and pour a few spoonfuls of stock at a time over vegetables. Cover tightly and allow to simmer in own juice until tender. Add more stock as needed.

When done, serve meat on platter with gravy and vegetables on top.

Serves 2-4.

3 pounds shin of veal

1/4 cup fat

1/2 teaspoon salt

2 cups seasoned stock

1/3 cup white wine

1 onion, cut in 8ths

2 parsley roots

1 bay leaf

2 cloves, heads removed

2 sprigs thyme

1/4 teaspoon pepper

2 stalks celery, cut in 2 inch strips

6 medium carrots, cut in 2 inch strips

4 large potatoes, cut in 2 inch strips

1/3 cup butter

1/2 teaspoon salt

1/4 to 1/2 cup unseasoned stock

ZILLI'S

Grandview Inn

Zilli's Grandview Inn
613 N. Grandview Blvd.
Waukesha, WI
(414) 549-3824

*Experience the thirty year tradition of culinary expertise at Zilli's Grandview Inn Restaurant in Waukesha. Rated ***** by the International Restaurant Rating Bureau, this white linen restaurant has often been called "the talk of the town." Executive Chef Thomas Voelske offers a variety of entrées pleasing to both the palate as well as the pocketbook. Offering weekly chef specials, Pasta and Lobster Nights and an award winning Friday Fish Fry.*

The featured recipe, Chicken Pecan, exemplifies the tradition of serving classic recipes from the Midwest with a contemporary flare. This dish is excellent when complemented by a full-bodied Chardonnay or Johannesberg Riesling from our well thought out wine list.

Enjoy dinner in our elegant dining room allowing our gracious servers to make you feel right at home. The Zilli Family has been preparing for your visit for three generations. Reservations are recommended. Open Tuesday through Sunday for dinner. Closed Mondays. The Grandview Inn is perfect for private occasions as well. Off premise catering provided by the award winning Ellen's Prestige Catering, one of the premier caterers in the state. Zilli's Grandview Inn... an unforgettable experience.

Fresh Tomato Concassé atop Pecan encrusted breast of Chicken set upon a tarn of Demi Glace.

Chicken Pecan

Rinse chicken breasts in cold water. Coat both sides in seasoned flour, make eggwash with eggs and milk. Dip floured chicken in eggwash and coat evenly with crushed pecans. In sauté pan heat clarified butter, pan sear chicken breasts evenly. Bake in 350 degree oven 15 minutes until internal temperature reaches 160 degrees or until juice from chicken runs clear when sliced.

Reduce chicken stock with all ingredients by one half. In pan, heat clarified butter, add tomatoes, green onion tops, fresh garlic. Deglaze pan with white wine and finish with whole butter.

Lace a small amount of Demi Glace in center of plate. Remove chicken and place over sauce. Top with Tomato Concassé. Garnish with fresh herbs.

Serves 2.

Chicken Pecan
2 boneless skinless 6 ounce chicken breasts

2 cups crushed pecans

1 cup flour-seasoned with salt and pepper

2 eggs

1 cup milk (2 percent)

1/4 cup clarified butter

Demi Glace
1 cup heavy chicken stock

1/2 teaspoon coarse black pepper

1 tablespoon tomato paste

1/2 tablespoon minced garlic

1/2 teaspoon chopped fresh tarragon

1 teaspoon chopped shallots

1/4 cup Marsala Wine

Tomato Concassé
1 cup peeled, seeded coarsely chopped fresh tomatoes

2 tablespoons green onion tops, chopped

1/2 cup Chablis Wine

1/2 tablespoon fresh garlic

2 tablespoons whole butter

1 tablespoon clarified butter

Benson's

509 W. Wisconsin
Milwaukee, WI
(414) 271-7250

"The place for steaks", Benson's specializes in a variety of USDA choice steaks, fresh fish, chops and seafoods. The steakhouse is a convenient site for dinner before your night out at the theatre, sporting events or to meet good friends. All guests are served a complimentary bucket of shrimp with their dinner entree order. Benson's is located on the avenue level inside the Milwaukee Hilton. Restaurant hours are Monday-Friday for lunch and Monday-Sunday for dinner.

savory veal chops grilled to perfection.

Grilled Veal Chop with Roquefort Green Peppercorn Sauce

Sprinkle veal chops with salt and pepper on both sides. Sear the veal by grilling it for 1 minute on each side. Continue grilling for 4-6 minutes on each side or until done to your taste. Meanwhile, in a skillet, sauté onions and garlic until transparent, about 1 minute. Add sherry and heating over medium heat, add Worcestershire sauce, mustard, demi-glaze, peppercorns, cheese and a pinch of salt, reduce heat to low and stir until cheese is melted. Add sour cream and reduce until sauce has the consistency of sour cream. Transfer the chops to individual plates and spoon sauce onto the plates to one side of the chop. Try a wild rice blend, grilled asparagus and red pepper as accompaniments.

4 3/4 inch thick veal chops

1 teaspoon salt

1/2 teaspoon ground black pepper

1/4 cup finely diced onions

1 tablespoon finely chopped garlic

1/2 cup sherry

1 tablespoon Worcestershire sauce

2 tablespoons Dijon-style mustard

1 cup veal demi-glaze

1/4 cup green peppercorns drained

3 ounces crumbled Roquefort cheese

1/2 cup sour cream

Shahrazad

Shahrazad Restaurant
2847 N. Oakland Ave.
Milwaukee, WI
(414) 964-5475

We proudly welcome you to the fresh, exciting taste of Shahrazad's traditional Middle Eastern Cuisine. A cuisine that will bring you a new global warming, the warming of hearts to each other. All of our ingredients and cooking methods are natural and authentic. We use savory blends of herbs and spices to create many uniquely seasoned tastes. Think of Shahrazad as your culinary window to the Middle East where you can enjoy an entirely different eating experience of entrees brought from across the world to your plate. We promise your appetite will be pleasantly fulfilled.

A savory blend of lamb meat, fresh herbs and grilled vegetables served with basmati rice and tahini.

Lamb Kefta Bel-Tahini

For the kefta, using meat grinder, grind all kefta ingredients. Mix very well. Salt & pepper to taste. Set aside.

For the sauce, use wire whisk to combine paste, lemon juice and water. Crush the garlic and add to the sauce. Bring to a boil on medium heat, constantly stirring. Keep sauce warm and correct your seasoning.

For the rice, heat olive oil in a sauce pan on low heat. Add rice and cook for approximately 2 minutes. Add chicken stock. Simmer on low heat for 30-35 minutes.

For the vegetables, alternate tomato, onion and pepper on wooden skewers. Salt & pepper. Grill until done.

For the dish, shape kefta into small oval shapes and grill on wooden skewers.

To assemble, put rice in the middle of dish. Pour warm sauce all around it. Alternate meat and vegetables around the rice. Garnish with parsley and pine nuts.

Kefta

1 pound of lean leg of lamb, boned

1/2 pound of lamb shoulder, boned

2 medium sized vidalia onions

5 cloves of garlic

10 sprigs of cilantro & parsley

1 leek (white part only)

Tahini Sauce

1/2 pound of "sesame seed paste"

2 cloves of garlic

juice from 3 lemons

1 cup ice water

Rice

3 ounces roasted pine nuts

1 cup basmati rice

1-1/2 cups chicken stock

3 teaspoons olive oil

salt & pepper to taste

cherry tomatoes

pearl onions

fresh jalapeño pepper

Smith Brothers Fish Shanty

100 N. Franklin
Port Washington, WI
(414) 377-2800

Established in 1934, Smith Bros. Fish Shanty "Wisconsin's Oldest Seafood Restaurant", is renowned throughout the Great Lakes for its fresh seafood and innovative entrees, as well as favorites like Oak Planked Fish and Mile High Lemon Meringue Pie. Daily features prepared by Chef Felicia Koepke are chosen for the freshest seafood, meats and produce available.

Guests may choose to dine in our elegant "Harbor Room" or outdoors (Memorial Day to Labor Day) on the second floor "Landing" overlooking beautiful Lake Michigan. There is also The Brew Pub for casual dining with Port Washington Brewing Co. beer served and brewed just behind the bar. Smith Bros. is also perfect for corporate and personal occasions, catering over 500 events a year in our four banquet rooms and on premise catering facilities that serve between 30 and 250 guests.

This featured recipe has become a favorite for shellfish aficionados. Sip a fine Chardonnay from our hand picked wine list, close your eyes, and this exquisite meal whisks you away to the small seaside port of La Rochelle, France.

...an enticing combination of tastes and textures, mingling tender sweet sea scallops, crisp vegetables and a Dill Havarti cream sauce enveloping puff pastry shells.

Scallops Vol au Vent

Bake the puff pastry shells per instructions, remove centers, and set aside. Prepare your Roux. Prepare the sauce in a heavy gauge sauce pot; combine cream, garlic, vegetable base, bitters, Worcestershire, and Tabasco and bring to a simmer. Add both cheeses a little at a time, allowing to completely melt while constantly whisking. Add the Roux and simmer slowly for 5 minutes. (To prevent lumping, be sure the Roux is warm when adding.) Finish by seasoning to taste with salt, pepper and nutmeg. Prepare the scallops, in a lightly oiled hot skillet, over medium high flame, quickly sauté vegetables and garlic until tender-crisp. Add scallops and sauté until medium rare (about 2 minutes). Add the dill havarti sauce and heat together for another minute or two. Place two puff pastry shells in the middle of each plate. Ladle the scallops & sauce into and around the shells. Serve with rice and garnish with fresh herbs and edible flowers.

15-20 large fresh sea scallops

6 ounces Fennel cut on bias

1 bunch of green onion cut on bias

1/2 pound asparagus cut on bias

2 ounces shredded carrots

1 dozen puff pastry shells

Dill Havarti Sauce

1 quart heavy cream

2 tablespoons minced fresh garlic

1-1/2 ounces vegetable base

2 tablespoons angostura bitters

2 tablespoons Worcestershire sauce

1 tablespoon Tabasco sauce

3 ounces parmesan cheese (grated)

1 pound dill havarti cheese (cubed)

4 ounces roux to thicken

dash of nutmeg

kosher salt to taste

white pepper to taste

Venice Club
1905 N. Calhoun Rd.
Brookfield, WI
(414) 786-8323

Relax in a warm, friendly atmosphere while you choose from our large menu of proven family favorites. Known for outstanding, quality food and specializing in over 25 fresh pasta dishes, the Venice Club remains "The Soul of Italy in the heart of Brookfield." We chose Chicken Garlic to feature because of its daring combination of flavors blended together to create an unforgettable taste experience. To perfectly complement this dish, serve with fresh Italian bread and seasoned olive oil, along with a fine Chardonnay. Our banquet rooms are perfect for your special occasion, with seating from 15 to 300. Off-premise catering can be provided as well.

Chicken Garlic

In a sauté pan melt butter and add olive oil. Add chopped onion and begin to sauté. Dredge chicken tenders through flour and add to sautéed items along with chopped garlic. Sauté two to three minutes and then add mushrooms and artichoke hearts, continue cooking another three to four minutes. Add sweet Marsala wine and reduce to about half. Add beef stock and simmer until reduced to half; adjust seasoning. Toss in cooked pasta, squeeze of lemon, toss and serve.

4 ounces chicken tenders

flour for dredging

1 tablespoon butter

1 tablespoon olive oil

2 tablespoons chopped onion

1 to 3 garlic cloves (chopped) depends on degree of flavor you are trying to achieve

3 medium canned artichoke hearts (quartered)

3 fresh mushrooms (chopped)

2 ounces Marsala wine

4 ounces beef stock (fresh or canned)

4 ounces angel hair pasta

squeeze of lemon

season with salt and pepper to taste

The Quilted Bear
N111 W18811 Mequon Rd.
Germantown, WI
(414) 255-1940

Since 1983, folks from all around have been enjoying the warm, friendly atmosphere of The Quilted Bear Restaurant. Our cozy decor of quilts, bears and picturesque surroundings that include natural wildlife, a man made pond and gazebo, make the perfect setting for a tranquil dining experience. Our Executive Chef, Daryl Zenke, along with our exceptional staff will welcome you and your guests. As Dennis Getto has stated in a restaurant write up, "Even Goldilocks would like The Quilted Bear" (July 96). The featured recipe, Veal Portifino, is one of our many veal specialties along with our wide menu selections of steaks, seafood and chicken entrees. We also feature two exciting dishes of bears in a blanket and Saturday evening alligator. The Quilted Bear also offers two beautiful banquet rooms which can accommodate up to 500 guests for weddings, business seminars or Christmas parties. Planning a special occasion? We will make you feel very BEARY welcome. Reservations are highly suggested. We are closed on Mondays. Call for more information.

Tender Veal Portifino to tempt your palate.

Veal Portifino

Mix bread crumbs, parsley, garlic, onion powder and seasoned salt together. Set aside. Heat cream, chicken base and pepper to boil. Add butter and flour mixture (roux) to thicken. Sauté scallops, shrimp, mushrooms and onions in salad oil until done and add to cream sauce. Pound veal with meat mallet between saran wrap to 1/8 inch thickness. Place in flour, then in egg wash (eggs and milk), then dip in breading mixture. Sauté veal with salad oil in a pan enough to lightly cover bottom. Sauté until golden brown. Flip and cook other side until golden brown. Place veal on a plate and cover with cream sauce.

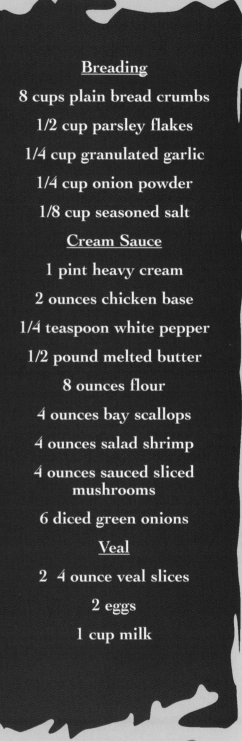

Breading
8 cups plain bread crumbs

1/2 cup parsley flakes

1/4 cup granulated garlic

1/4 cup onion powder

1/8 cup seasoned salt

Cream Sauce
1 pint heavy cream

2 ounces chicken base

1/4 teaspoon white pepper

1/2 pound melted butter

8 ounces flour

4 ounces bay scallops

4 ounces salad shrimp

4 ounces sauced sliced mushrooms

6 diced green onions

Veal
2 4 ounce veal slices

2 eggs

1 cup milk

The Bangkok Orchid

Bangkok Orchid
2239 N. Prospect Ave.
Milwaukee, WI
(414) 223-3333

Magically transport yourself from Milwaukee's East Side to the exotic Far East. It has been our dream at the Bangkok Orchid to recreate the joy, color and pageantry which typifies the Thai way of life. From the artwork that adorns the walls to the artful presentation of your meal, authenticity is our paramount concern. All ingredients and cooking methods are identical to those used in Thai kitchens, where recipes are lovingly passed from generation to generation. We know you will love Thai cuisine. But far beyond the meal itself, we hope to make your entire dining experience an event to be savored.

This is a very traditional Thai noodle dish from the Bangkok area of Thailand. It could be described as the "Thai hamburger" and is available at all Thai restaurants throughout Bangkok. For this flavorful dish we combine rice noodles, stir fried in a delicate sauce, with spices and fresh ingredients to create a delightful combination that your palate will truly enjoy.

Pudt Thai Noodles

Soak the packages of noodles in cool water for at least one hour (overnight is best).

Drain, then soak half the bean sprouts in water.

Cut chives in half, save bottom for garnish and cut top half into one-inch strips.

In a wok, heat cooking oil and fry garlic until light brown.

Optional: (Add any sautéed meat, shrimp, crushed nuts, eggs or mushrooms (black or straw are best) to suit your taste.)

In our recipe we used 1 pound chicken, broccoli tops, carrot coins, vidalia onions, and tofu, from Simple Soyman. (The vegetables should be steamed in a steamer first so they are half cooked.) The tofu should be freshly squeezed, but not pre-cooked.

Add enough pre-soaked noodles to feed up to four people. Add them to the wok and let them cook at high heat. Then add previously soaked bean sprouts, fish sauce, vinegar, tamarind, and then finally the sugar.

Stir fry until noodles are brown. Add chives, and turn over a few times.

Place on serving plate, and garnish with bean sprouts and chives.

Served with fresh diced chili peppers and vinegar sauce, or sprinkle with freshly ground cayenne pepper, if you like your food spicy.

1 pound Thai Rice Stick noodles - use the ones which are 3 millimeters wide or medium size.

1 cup of fresh bean sprouts

5 stalks of chives

1 teaspoon of minced garlic

1/4 cup vegetable oil

2 tablespoons Thai fish sauce. (Nam Pla)

3 tablespoons granulated sugar

1 tablespoon vinegar

1 tablespoon tamarind juice (Use fresh juice from 1/2 lime if no tamarind)

3-5 finely chopped cayenne peppers, soaked in 2 tablespoons of vinegar

1/2 cup broccoli tops

1/2 cup carrot coins

1/2 cup vidalia onions, sliced

1/2 cup freshly pressed tofu, cubed

Cafe Knickerbocker

Cafe Knickerbocker
1030 E. Juneau
Milwaukee, WI
(414) 272-0011

The Cafe Knickerbocker - an eclectic array of food at affordable prices. The kind of restaurant where comfort is essential for all guests, whether on a date or with a group. The perfect atmosphere in a gallery setting with excellent service. It will make your dining experience one that will bring you back again. Cafe Knickerbocker, the forerunner of fine, reasonable dining.

A delightful dish complemented with saffron rice and grilled portobello mushrooms.

Sunflower Crusted Sea Bass with Roasted Acorn Squash Sauce

Preheat Oven to 375 Degrees

To Prepare the Acorn Squash:
Cut the acorn squash in half and remove the seeds. Place on a baking sheet with a small amount of water and bake in the 375 degree oven till soft, approximately 40 minutes. In a saucepan add a small amount of oil and sauté the shallots and garlic until they are translucent. Add the orange juice, chicken stock, ginger, honey and acorn squash. Let the sauce come to a boil and simmer for fifteen minutes. Remove the ginger and purée the sauce in a blender. Adjust consistency with chicken stock if it is too thick and season with salt and pepper.

For Crust:
Combine bread crumbs and sunflower seeds in a medium size bowl.

To Prepare the Sea Bass:
Season the sea bass by sprinkling lightly with salt and pepper. Place the sunflower crust in a pie tin. Firmly press the sea bass in the sunflower crust on both sides. Heat a large sauté pan or two smaller pans on medium heat. You do not want to crowd the sea bass by placing it too close together. When the pan is hot, place the coated sea bass in the pan and cook until golden brown. Turn the fish over and place in the preheated oven to bake for ten minutes, then take out of the oven and let rest for three to five minutes. Place two ounces of sauce on each plate and place the sea bass on the sauce.

The sea bass is mild white flaky fish that lends itself to almost any preparation. At the Cafe Knickerbocker, we compliment this dish with saffron rice and grilled portobello mushrooms. This sea bass preparation could also be accompanied by roasted potatoes and asparagus.

4   6 ounce sea bass fillets

1 cup fresh bread crumbs

1 1/2 cups sunflower seeds coarsely chopped

1 medium acorn squash

2 shallots

1 teaspoon puréed garlic

1 half inch piece of fresh ginger

2 tablespoons honey

2 cups chicken stock

1/4 cup orange juice

salt and pepper

West Bank Cafe
732 E. Burleigh St.
Milwaukee, WI
(414) 562-5555

WestBankCafe

At West Bank Cafe, Vietnamese cuisine has become a fascinating art of blending traditional cooking with a flavor of Chinese intrigue and a touch of French sophistication. The melange of the best ingredients with creative methods makes palate-watering dishes with tempting flavor and breath-taking decoration a reality. The featured recipe, Grilled Lemon Grass Chicken, offers the unique combination of excellence in taste, flavor, and presentation. The nutritious dish promotes a balanced health-conscious diet and the appetite is well enhanced when accompanied by a fine Chardonnay.

West Bank Cafe is consistently ranked as one of the Top Thirty Restaurants in the Milwaukee metropolitan area by The Milwaukee Journal Sentinel. It makes the list, year after year, as the Top Twenty Five Best Restaurants, and was voted the Best Atmosphere of dining establishments by the Milwaukee Magazine. The cozy restaurant was also featured several times on local CBS and FOX television stations. The executive chef, recipient of the Top Two Thousand Chefs of America Award by the National Executive Chefs Association, has been preparing award-winning entrees to satisfied patrons for more than seventeen consecutive years. Open for dinner seven days a week.

A savory blend of grilled chicken on fresh lettuce and garnished vegetable, served with steamy rice.

Grilled Lemon Grass Chicken

In a shallow pan large enough to hold chicken in a single layer, add chicken, brandy, turmeric, salt, honey, all-spice, chili powder, and black pepper together. Mix well. Cover and marinate overnight in the refrigerator.

Add freshly minced lemon grass to coat chicken all sides before grilling.

Two ways to prepare:

1. Build a medium-hot fire on a charcoal Hibachi. Grill chicken, turn over occasionally. The chicken is done when chicken strips are lightly charred. The cooking time is 10 minutes. Mix well in scallion sauce*.

2. Preheat a large sauté pan to 400 degrees. Add vegetable oil. Add chicken to pan forming a single layer. Reduce heat and cover for 3 minutes. Turn chicken over, then cook for 3 more minutes. Watch for lightly charred look of the chicken.

Add scallions. Mix well.

Note the sure sign of thoroughly cooked chicken: the juice appears clear when the flesh is pierced with a fork or a skewer.

Serve on a bed of shredded lettuce and garnish the surrounding with sweet and sour vegetables**.

Enjoy grilled lemon grass chicken with Jasmine steamed rice.

*Scallion sauce: Preheat sauté pan to 300 degrees. Pour in vegetable oil. Then add scallions to hot oil. Stir lightly. Turn off heat.

**Sweet and sour vegetables: Mix some shredded green cabbage and carrot with pickled daikon, then add a little salt, one part of sugar to two parts of vinegar. Mix well. Set overnight in the refrigerator.

1 pound lean chicken breast fillet, cut into strips

1 tablespoon brandy

1 teaspoon turmeric

1 teaspoon salt

1 tablespoon honey or sugar

1/2 teaspoon all-spice seasoning

Optional: a dash of chili powder and black pepper

2 tablespoons minced fresh lemon grass

2 tablespoons chopped scallions

1 tablespoon vegetable oil

Saz's State House

5539 W. State St.
Milwaukee, WI
(414) 453-2410

Experience "The Finest" at Milwaukee's premier BBQ restaurant and sports bar. Come visit and see why Milwaukeeans continue to vote Saz's as "The Best in Town" for BBQ Ribs. In business for well over 20 years, Proprietor Stephen P. Sazama has a knack for entertaining his customers tastes. Though Ribs are obviously the house specialty, he also serves a wide variety of other entrees on the menu. In addition to his famed restaurant, Mr. Sazama has other ventures such as an Off Premise Catering Business, an Off Premise Festivals Concessions Business, Retail Business for his BBQ products, and even food service operations at a golf country club, and in the downtown Grand Avenue Mall.

The featured recipe is wild with tantalizing flavors. By the time you are done with your meal (believe me, your plate will be clean) you won't be able to figure out which was better, the Ribs or the Shrimp.

Saz's offers a comfortable, not stuffy, atmosphere with a sophisticated sports bar feel. Choose to dine in either of the two dining rooms, or on nice summer days, watch the trains go by at the outdoor beer garden. For that before or after dinner drink, take your pick between the unique round bar or the "new" bar. Reservations are accepted for parties of eight or larger.

BBQ Ribs and Jumbo Cajun Shrimp

Here's how you can make Saz's famous ribs (for four) right at home. Cut racks in half and put sideways in a 5 to 6 inch deep pan. Cover ribs with liquid smoke, white pepper and water so the liquid is 3/4 of the way up on the ribs. Bake ribs covered tightly in a 350 degree oven for approximately 2 1/2 hours. Ribs will be done when the meat is easily separated from the bones. When ribs are finished cooking, drain and refrigerate until cool. Now all that is left is to finish them on your charcoal or gas grill.

Grilling recommendation:
Place ribs top side down on hot grill until that particular side is hot and sizzling. Sauce that side and flip. Repeat to other side and serve.

Sauté shrimp in Tabasco, Worcestershire and 3 tablespoons of butter mixture briefly (about 1 minute on high flame) so the shrimp will absorb the mixture. Set aside in a shallow baking dish. Melt 1/4 pound of butter in saucepan. Stir in salt, chili powder, parsley, garlic, black pepper, cayenne pepper, onion, bell pepper and curry powder. Simmer for about 4 minutes. Pour Tabasco, Worcestershire and butter mixture over shrimp in baking dish. Bake for 20 minutes at 350 degrees. Try serving this with your favorite pasta. Recipe serves 4. Enjoy!

BBQ Ribs
2 1 1/2 pound racks baby back pork ribs (skinned)
1/2 cup liquid smoke
2 teaspoons white pepper
water to submerse
Saz's original or sassy BBQ sauce

Jumbo Cajun Shrimp
16 jumbo shrimp (10 to 15 count)
1 tablespoon Worcestershire
3 tablespoons butter or margarine
1/4 pound butter or margarine
1/8 teaspoon salt
1/2 teaspoon chili powder
1 tablespoon fresh parsley
1/2 tablespoon minced fresh garlic
1 lemon wedge
1/4 teaspoon black pepper
1/4 teaspoon cayenne pepper
1/4 medium onion finely chopped
1/4 bell pepper finely chopped
1 teaspoon curry powder

Jimmy D's Steak House
15108 W. Bluemound Rd.
Milwaukee, WI
(414)774-9100

A casual, yet fine dining environment, with an extensive top rail and a substantial wine list, Jimmy D's is being developed and advertised as Milwaukee's newest Steak House. However, we add a French flair to things and aren't afraid to try something new and off the beaten path, like great roast duckling at a steak house!

Chef Roger's signature roast duckling.

Roast Wisconsin Duckling a la Orange

Rinse and trim excess fat and skin from duck. Save all giblets, and neck bone, cut first wing joint off. In deep braising pan put all wing and neck bones in bottom to prevent duck from sticking, place breast side up. Pour soy sauce over entire duck, making sure all skin is covered thoroughly. Cover with foil. Roast at 375 degrees for 1 hour. Pour all drippings off. Reserve for sauce. Put 1 quart water in pan, roast uncovered for 1 hour or until golden brown.

Grand Marnier Orange Sauce:
In saucepan heat 1 quart chicken stock, 3 cups orange juice, 3 ounces Grand Marnier, 1 teaspoon garlic, 1/2 teaspoon white pepper. Heat to soft boil. In separate saucepan heat duck drippings. Thicken with all-purpose flour to the consistency of paste. Cook over low heat for 5 minutes. Slowly add to stock to desired thickness. Cook over low heat for 30 minutes. Strain and adjust seasoning.

1 quart chicken stock

3 cups orange juice

3 ounces Grand Marnier

1 whole duckling 3-5 pounds

all-purpose flour

1/8 cup soy sauce

1 teaspoon white pepper

1/2 - 1 teaspoon garlic

Thai Palace
838 N. Old World 3rd St.
Milwaukee, WI
(414) 224-7076

Come experience an authentic Thai evening in an elegant atmosphere. You will enjoy the rich cobalt blue decor as well as a wonderfully unique menu. Rated the best Thai food in Milwaukee and located downtown across from the Hyatt, Thai Palace is the perfect place for dinner before or after your favorite play or sporting event. We look forward to showing you our gracious hospitality. We are also open for lunch. Reservations recommended.

Breaded veal slices topped with sautéed mushrooms, onions, and green peppers, crowned with mozzarella cheese and topped with tomato sauce.

Veal Leonardo

Dip veal slices in egg wash, then bread crumbs, press down to coat veal on both sides. Sauté mushrooms, onions, and green peppers al dente in a little olive oil. Season with oregano, basil, garlic powder, and crushed red pepper. Bake breaded veal slices in oven with a little olive oil at 350 degrees for 10 minutes. Put sautéed vegetables over veal slices, top with mozzarella cheese. Place under broiler to melt cheese and top with tomato sauce. Serve with a side of mostaccioli.

2 3 ounce center cut veal leg slices

green pepper slices

sliced onions

mushrooms

Italian seasoned breadcrumbs

mozzarella cheese slices

seasoned tomato sauce (or your own spaghetti sauce)

egg wash (1 cup milk with 1 beaten egg)

olive oil

oregano

basil

garlic powder

crushed red pepper

Fountain Blue

Fountain Blue
5133 S. Lake Dr.
Cudahy, WI
(414) 481-8222

There is an obvious warm atmosphere at the Fountain Blue where the congenial staff makes friends quickly with their guests, who feel at home in an establishment that not only boasts of some of the best cuisine in Milwaukee, but also the friendliest service. Surround yourself with stained glass windows, sit beside our flowing fountain, select a fine wine from our cruvinet or micro brew from a menu of 55 beers. Banquets up to 100. Reservations recommended on weekends. Closed Mondays. Heavenly Sunday brunch.

Enjoy the authentic flavors of this wonderful Polish dish.

Krakow Stuffed Tenderloin

Pound tenderloin filet with meat mallet until 1/4 inch thick. Then salt and pepper filet to taste. Brown Polish sausage. Place 2 slices of Swiss cheese on flattened filet. Place Polish sausage on top of cheese at end of filet. Fold 1/2 of filet over top of Polish sausage. Then take each side of filet and fold over the sides of sausage, then continue rolling. Whip eggs and milk together for an egg wash. Take stuffed filet, dredge in flour, dip in egg wash and coat with bread crumbs until completely covered. Brown all sides in skillet with hot vegetable oil. Bake in preheated 350 degree oven for 15-20 minutes until desired doneness. Serve with beef gravy if you like, fresh veggies and your favorite side dish.

2 6 ounce tenderloin filets

6 ounces bulk Polish sausage

4 slices Swiss cheese

salt and pepper

6 cups bread crumbs

4 cups flour

6 eggs beaten

1 cup of milk

cup vegetable oil

Louise's Trattoria

801 N. Jefferson
Milwaukee, WI
(414) 273-4224

Visit our vibrant trattoria featuring eclectic Italian and California cuisine. Handmade pasta, gnocchi, tortelloni and ravioli are specialties, along with hand-tossed pizzas boasting a myriad of gourmet toppings. Start with an antipasti of steamed mussels, roasted portobello mushrooms or an insalata of organic baby lettuces with goat cheese, pine nuts and sundried tomatoes. Entrées are worth sharing. Three citrus-grilled chicken, tagliolini alla pescatora or penne rigate with asparagus, sundried tomatoes, and mushrooms all offer an interesting variety of flavors.

An outdoor patio is available for those who would like to lunch in the sun or dine under the stars while enjoying a selection from our extensive wine list. Delivery and catering are services offered as well as a wonderful Sunday Brunch.

A unique flavor, blending garlic, red chilies, green onion, roasted red bell peppers and fresh oregano.

Jumbo Shrimp and Pasta

Season shrimp with salt and pepper. Add shrimp to the pan. Let shrimp brown on one side for 30 seconds, then turn shrimp over for another 30 seconds. Add chopped garlic, crushed chilies, oregano and green onions. Cook for one minute. Then add roasted red peppers. Add wine, reduce by 1/2, then add butter. Toss with cooked tagliolini. Serve on a large dinner plate with parsley garnish.

1 ounce garlic oil

5 shrimp, 16/20

1/4 teaspoon chilis (crushed red)

1/2 tablespoon garlic (chopped)

2 tablespoons green onion

1 tablespoon oregano

1 1/2 tablespoons roasted red pepper

2 ounces Chardonnay

1 1/2 tablespoons butter

1 nest tagliolini

1 parsley sprig

100

Measurements & Equivalents

3 teaspoons
1 tablespoon

2 quarts
1/2 gallon

8 egg yolks
1/2 cup

4 tablespoons
1/4 cup

4 quarts
1 gallon

1 cup raw rice
3-4 cups cooked

4 ounces
1/2 cup

1 stick of butter
1/2 cup

1 medium lemon
2-3 tablespoons juice

8 ounces
1 cup

1 pound of brown sugar
2 1/4 cups (packed)

1 pound of seedless raisins
3 cups

2 cups
1 pint

1 pound of powdered sugar
3 1/2 cups (sifted)

2 ounces chocolate chips
1/3 cup

2 pints
1 quart

8 egg whites
1 cup

6 ounces chocolate chips
1 cup

Substitutions

1 ounce bittersweet chocolate
use 3 tablespoons cocoa plus
1 1/2 teaspoons fat or 1 tablespoon
liquid butter buds

1 cup cake flour
1 cup minus 1 tablespoon
all-purpose flour

1 cup self-rising flour
1 cup all-purpose flour,
1/2 tablespoon baking soda,
1 1/2 teaspoons baking powder,
and 1/2 teaspoon light salt

1 teaspoon baking powder
1/4 teaspoon baking soda plus
1/2 cup buttermilk or sour milk
(to replace 1/2 cup of the liquid
in the recipe)

1 teaspoon dry mustard
1 tablespoon prepared mustard

1 package active dry yeast
1 cake compressed yeast

oil
use applesauce, cup for cup

1 small onion
1 teaspoon onion powder or
tablespoon minced dried
onion, rehydrated

1 teaspoon grated lemon peel
1/2 teaspoon lemon extract

chicken broth
use honey, cup for cup

1 cup white sugar
1 cup brown sugar or 2 cups sifted
powdered sugar or 1 cup molasses
plus 1/4 to 1/2 baking soda. Reduce
liquid by 1/4 cup

1 tablespoon cornstarch
(for thickening)
2 tablespoons all-purpose flour

1 clove garlic
1/8 teaspoon garlic powder or
1/8 teaspoon minced dried garlic
or 1/2 teaspoon minced
garlic in a jar

1 cup buttermilk
1 tablespoon lemon juice or vinegar
plus skim milk to make 1 cup

2 cups tomato sauce
use 3/4 cup tomato paste
plus 1 cup water

Who Makes America's Finest Sausage?

These Guys Do.

Herb Chart

Allspice-
Meatball appetizers, beef stew, pot roast, ham, lamb, oysters

Basil-
Turtle soup, meat loaf, venison, halibut, goose, duck, turkey

Bay Leaf-
Beef stew, fish chowders, spareribs, shrimp, crab, seafood casseroles

Cloves-
Beef soup, ham, pork roasts, baked fish, roasted chicken

Curry Powder-
Clam chowder, chicken soup, lamb, veal, shrimp, baked fish

Garlic-
Barbecue sauce, steaks, stews, Italian & French meat dishes, chicken, fish

Ginger-
Boiled beef, lamb, veal, baked or sauteed chicken, cornish hen

Marjoram-
Pot roast, stews, lamb, scallops, broiled fish

Mustard-
Meat dips, ham sauces, beef-onion soup, lamb

Nutmeg-
Cream of chicken soup, salisbury steak, meat loaf, chicken

Oregano-
Meat sauces, beef, pork, veal, lamb, Swiss steak, fried chicken

Paprika-
Egg dishes, chicken, potato salad, stews, goulash

Rosemary-
Chicken or meat soups, veal stews, lamb, creamed shellfish

Saffron-
Poultry stuffing, chicken soup stock, lamb, veal, sausage, chicken, halibut

Sage-
Meat sauces and gravies, chowders, cold roast beef, stews, pork dishes

Tarragon-
Meat sauces, meat canape mixtures, veal, sweet breads, turkey, game chicken, chicken salads

Thyme-
Meat sauces, chowders, oyster stew

Glossary

Anchovies-

Small, silvery saltwater fish that come from the Mediterranean and the coastlines of southern Europe. They are usually filleted, salted and canned in oil. To alleviate saltiness, soak in water for 30 minutes, drain and pat dry with paper towel.

Beans-

Beans can be broken down into two categories - fresh and dried. The three most common fresh bean varieties are green beans, lima beans and fava beans. Popular dried beans include black beans, chickpeas, kidney beans and white beans. Dried beans must usually be soaked in water before cooking.

Bell Peppers-

They have a mild, sweet taste and crisp, juicy flesh. Most are deep green in color and are available year-round. Other varieties are seasonal and include yellow, red, orange, brown and purple.

Butter-

Butter may be salted or unsalted. For best cooking results, use unsalted. Butter quickly absorbs flavor, so it should be wrapped airtight for storage.

Capers-

Capers are small buds of a bush common to the Mediterranean. The buds are sun-dried and pickled in a vinegar brine. They can be found packed in brine or salted and sold in bulk. Rinse before using to remove excess salt.

Chile Peppers-

Chiles come in more than 200 varieties. They vary from mild to extremely hot in taste and vary in coloring. For best cooking results, choose chiles with deep, vivid colors. Wear rubber gloves when preparing to avoid burning of the eyes. If no gloves are used, be sure to wash hands thoroughly after preparation.

Cornstarch-

Generally used as a thickening agent in a variety of foods. You may want to mix it with a small amount of cold liquid or a granular solid before stirring it in with a hot mixture. This will help prevent the formation of lumps.

Eggs-

Large eggs should be used when preparing the recipes in this book. The color of the eggshell does not affect the taste or nutritional value. Always refrigerate. For best flavor and quality, use eggs within one week.

Flours-

All-purpose flour is most commonly used for baking. Its two basic forms are bleached and unbleached. Bleached flour produces a tender result whereas unbleached more crisp. Flour greased baking pans to help remove goods more easily.

Mushrooms-

There are thousands of varieties of mushrooms. The cultivated white mushroom has a mild, earthy flavor and is readily available. Other varieties include the shiitake, morel, puffball and portobello. Store fresh mushrooms with cool air circulating around them. When using them whole, use mushrooms of equal size to ensure even cooking. Before using, wipe with a damp paper towel or rinse them with cold water and dry thoroughly.

Mustard, Dijon-

A pale, grayish-yellowish mustard originally made in Dijon, France. It is made from brown or black mustard seeds, white wine or wine vinegar, unfermented grape juice and various seasonings. Its flavor ranges from mild to hot.

Nuts-

Any of a variety of dry fruits that are rich and mellow in flavor. Some popular nuts include almonds, cashews, chestnuts, macadamias, pecans, peanuts, pistachios, pine nuts and walnuts. When possible, buy nuts that are plump, crisp and uniform in size and color. Nuts should always be purchased and used as fresh as possible for best flavor. Store them in an airtight container in a cool place.

Oils-

Oils are used for cooking, baking and enhancing the texture and flavor of foods. Oils generally come from vegetable sources. Varieties include almond, olive, extra virgin olive, light olive, coconut, canola, safflower, corn and peanut. Most oils should be stored in a cool, dark place.

Olives-

Small, oily fruit native to the Mediterranean area. There are many varieties that vary in size and color. Black olives are cured in brine or salt and are generally packed in olive oil or vinegar. You may store unopened olives for up to two years at room temperature.

Glossary

Onions-

The two main categories of onions are green and dry. Green onions, also known as scallions, have a sweet, mild flavor because they have a high water and sugar content. Dry onions have a juicy flesh covered with multiple layers of dry skin. All varieties of onions may be braised, boiled, steamed, baked, sautéed, scalloped, fried or grilled. Sauté onions to soften their texture and enrich their taste. Also, you may want to simmer onions in wine or broth instead of butter in order to lower the fat content. Freeze the onion for 20 minutes before you are prepared to chop them to alleviate any tearing of the eyes.

Pastas-

A wide variety of noodles made from an Italian type of dough that is semolina combined with water or milk. Pasta that is made with flour and eggs is generally referred to as noodles. Spaghetti and macaroni are two of the most popular of the varieties. Conchiglie is shell-shaped; farfalle is bow-shaped; and rotelle is shaped like little corkscrews. Ravioli and tortellini have fillings, often meat and cheese. Green pasta is colored with spinach; red with tomato or beet juice; and squid ink is used to create charcoal gray. Fresh pasta cooks faster than dried, but is highly perishable. Use light sauces for delicate pastas and heavy sauces for sturdy pastas.

Shellfish-

Shellfish include a variety of underwater creatures. Be sure that all lobsters are alive when you purchase them. Lobster is best when it is broiled or boiled. Shrimp comes in a variety of colors including shades of red, brown, yellow, gray and green. Texture and flavor does not vary much among shrimp. Boil, fry

or grill them for the best flavor. Crab meat is sweet and succulent and is best when fried, boiled, steamed or used in a dish. Mussels have a sweet flavored meat and are best when steamed, fried or baked. There are two types of scallops - bay and sea. It is best to cook them for a short period of time. Scallops may be sautéed, grilled, broiled or poached. They are often used in a variety of salads, stews and soups.

Soy Sauce-

A dark, salty sauce made from soy beans, wheat, salt and water and is a main ingredient in Asian cooking. It has a shelf life of many months when stored in a cool, dark place. It is used to flavor a variety of foods and is often a tasty table condiment.

Spices-

Sweet or savory seasonings obtained from the bark, dried seeds, roots, fruit, buds or stems of a variety of plants and trees. Spices should always be used sparingly. Allspice is brown in color and may be purchased either ground or whole. It is used for all types of cooking. Cardamom is a member of the ginger family. It has a strong aroma, with a warm, sweet flavor. It can be used to flavor dishes such as stews and curries. Ceylon cinnamon is mildly sweet, whereas cassia (the most common cinnamon) has a strong, slightly bittersweet taste. It is commonly used as a flavoring for cooking sweet dishes. Cloves can be used to flavor with a touch of sweetness and has a strong, spicy aroma. Mace is used to flavor all different kinds of foods. Nutmeg has a warm, sweet and spicy flavor. It is a delicious additive used in baked goods, milk-based foods, fruits and vegetables. Paprika is a seasoning used in savory dishes. Its flavor ranges from mild to hot.

Pepper is the most common spice. The peppercorn comes in three varieties - black, white and green. Saffron is a golden-orange spice and is mainly used to flavor and tint food.

Sugars-

There are many types of sugars used to sweeten various recipes. Sugar not only sweetens, it can also make dough tender, add stability to mixtures, brown the surfaces of baked goods and help preserve foods. Granulated (white) sugar is the most common sugar used for cooking. It is highly refined and made from beets or cane. Confectioners' sugar is finely pulverized with a small amount of cornstarch added to prevent clumping. It is also used to make icings, candy and decorative coatings on desserts. Brown sugar, light or dark, is white sugar that has been combined with molasses. It tastes rich and has a soft texture. The darker the brown, the more molasses flavoring.

Tomatoes-

There are dozens of tomato varieties available, but for cooking, beefsteak and plum tomatoes are the best. Beefsteak tomatoes have a delicious bright red, slightly elliptical-shape and are good for eating raw or for cooking. Plum tomatoes are egg-shaped and are red or yellow in color, and can be purchased canned for cooking. When selecting, choose firm, well-shaped tomatoes that smell good and have a deep color. The perfect tomato should have no blemishes, be heavy for its size and give slightly when pressed in the palm of your hand. Store ripe tomatoes at room temperature and use them as quickly as possible. They last only a few days. Never refrigerate. Cold temperatures make them lose flavor and develop a pulpy flesh.

Restaurant Index

Recipe Index